VEDĀNTA
And its Philosophical Development

Contemporary Researches in
Hindu Philosophy & Religion
(ISSN 0971-9628)

1. Idealistic Thought in Indian Philosophy; by Shuchita C. Divatia (ISBN 81-246-0021-X)
2. Karma and Reincarnation: The Vedāntic Perspective; by Muni Narayana Prasad (ISBN 81-246-0022-8)
3. Stonemill and Bhakti: From the Devotion of Peasant Women to the Philosophy of Swamies; by Guy Poitevin and Hema Rairkar (ISBN 81-246-0059-7)
4. Śaivism: Some Glimpses; by G.V. Tagare (ISBN 81-246-0076-7)
5. Advaita: A Conceptual Analysis; by A. Ramamurty (ISBN 81-246-0067-8)
6. Mind-Body Dualism: A Philosophic Investigation; by Alpana Chakraborty (ISBN 81-246-0071-6)
7. Hinduism and Scientific Quest; by T.R.R. Iyengar (ISBN 81-246-0077-5)
8. Indra and Other Vedic Deities — A Euhemeristic Study; by Uma Chakravarty (ISBN 81-246-0080-5)
9. Brahma-Vāda: Doctrine of Śrī Vallabhācārya; by G.V. Tagare (ISBN 81-246-0112-7)
10. The Science of Enlightenment: Enlightenment, Liberation and God — A Scientific Explanation; by Nitin Trasi (ISBN 81-246-0130-5)
11. Retrieval of Sāṁkhya History: An Ascent from Dawn to Meridian; by Lallanji Gopal (ISBN 81-246-0143-7)
12. The Philosophical Foundations of Hinduism; by A. Ramamurty (ISBN 81-246-0163-1)
13. The Eternal Hinduism; by Baidyanath Saraswati (ISBN 81-246-0249-2)
14. Vedānta and its Philosophical Development; by A. Ramamurty (ISBN 81-246-0347-2)

Contemporary Researches in Hindu Philosophy & Religion, no. 14

VEDĀNTA
And its Philosophical Development

A. Ramamurty

D.K. Printworld (P) Ltd.
New Delhi

Cataloging in Publication Data — DK
[Courtesy: D.K. Agencies (P) Ltd. <docinfo@dkagencies.com>]

Ramamurty, A. (Aryasomayajula), 1935-
Vedānta and its philosophical development / A. Ramamurty.
(Contemporary researches in Hindu philosophy & religion, no. 14).
p. 23 cm.
Includes bibliographical references (p.)
Includes index.
ISBN 8124603472

1. Vedanta. 2. Philosophy, Hindu. I. Title. II. Series: Contemporary researches in Hindu philosophy & religion, no. 14.

DDC 181.48 21

ISBN 81-246-0347-2
First published in India in 2006

Published and printed by:
D.K. Printworld (P) Ltd.
Regd. Office: 'Sri Kunj', F-52, Bali Nagar
New Delhi-110 015
Phones: (011) 2545-3975, 2546-6019; *Fax*: (011) 2546-5926
E-mail: dkprintworld@vsnl.net
Website: www.dkprintworld.com

Preface

THE problem of reconciliation of mutually incompatible statements of the Upaniṣads, on all important problems discussed in the Upaniṣads, has attracted the attention of almost all the major philosophers of Vedānta. The Upaniṣadic statements in which the nature of *Brahman* is indicated are not compatible with the statements which express the nature and reality of the world of empirical experience. They even contradict each other. Thus, the basic problem in developing the philosophy of the Upaniṣads or in interpreting them is how to reconcile the reality of *Brahman*, as indicated or shown in the Upaniṣads, with that of the world of empirical experience, or vice versa. Several problems of philosophic importance are analysed and, discussed in the Upaniṣads, and, different views which are not consistent with each other are freely expressed in them. And we do not find in the Upaniṣads any view or doctrine being endorsed by them. However, what is commonly expressed in all the texts of the Upaniṣads is a world-view or an ontological vision. And one significant thing about the Upaniṣads is that they are mostly pedagogic in character, and have adopted or developed several literary devices and methods to serve the purpose of instruction. The Upaniṣads are not revelations in the sense that they give us something definite and final for our acceptance on faith. They teach us something which is not unknown to anyone. Their main object is to reveal the nature of the divine or *Brahman* as it reveals itself at the human level or within the reality of man (*adhyātma*).

In their attempts to reconcile the reality of *Brahman* with that of the world of empirical experience almost all the philosophers of Vedānta have resorted to reason. Bādarāyaṇa, the first person to develop a coherent philosophy on the basis of the Upaniṣads, has recognized the role and value of reason in understanding the philosophy of the Upaniṣads. As we do not find in the Upaniṣads any definite or conclusive statement or view on most of the basic problems, we have to depend upon reason for understanding the philosophy of the Upaniṣads. It is a different thing whether reason can really help in reconciling the Upaniṣadic statements or in understanding the meaning of the Upaniṣads. But all the interpreters of Vedānta have resorted to reason in understanding the philosophy of the Upaniṣads. They have developed rational justification in support of their philosophical or metaphysical positions, and used reason freely in criticizing the rival positions. In this process several arguments which are subtle and cogent are developed. However, most of the interpreters who have shown philosophic zeal and critical spirit in understanding and criticizing the rival positions and arguments are not so critical about their own positions. Thus, the Vedāntins who came after Śaṅkara, and have made his position (Advaita) their *pūrva-pakṣa*, have not, however, tried to understand their own positions as critically as they have tried to understand the rival position.

This is an attempt, though brief but comprehensive, to understand the philosophic aspect or side of the development of Vedānta. I have chosen for the purpose five major philosophers of Vedānta who represent different approaches, and, the discussion is limited to their ways of reconciling the reality of *Brahman* with that of the world of empirical experience.

I take this opportunity to thank Sri Susheel K. Mittal, the director, D.K. Printworld (P) Ltd., New Delhi for his friendly attitude, and for publishing this work.

Hyderabad
5th Sept. 2005.

A. Ramamurty

Contents

1

Introduction

Among the systems of Indian philosophy it is the Vedānta which has a history of continuous philosophic development. Bādarāyaṇa, the author of the *Brahma-Sūtras*, was the first to develop a coherent system of philosophy based on the Upaniṣads, or the *Brahma-Sūtras* marks the beginning of the philosophic development of Vedānta. However, Bādarāyaṇa is not an interpreter of the Upaniṣads in the usual sense; he did not comment on the Upaniṣads directly. The object of Bādarāyaṇa in developing a philosophy of the Upaniṣads is two-fold. Firstly, to present the thought or wisdom of the Upaniṣads in a systematic and coherent manner so as to make it, as far as possible, meaningful to rational understanding of man, and secondly to defend it against the criticisms of rival schools of philosophy, especially Sāṁkhya and Buddhism. He also tried to present the philosophy of the Upaniṣads as more meaningful and valid in comparison to other systems of philosophy.

However, the major problem faced by almost all the philosophers of Vedānta is how to reconcile and harmonize the various Upaniṣadic texts and statements which are not compatible with each other. The Upaniṣadic statements on most of the important problems discussed in the Upaniṣads are not compatible with each other, they even conflict with each other. The mutual conflict among the statements of the Upaniṣads is a major problem in understanding and developing the philosophy of the Upaniṣads. What is stated at one place in the Upaniṣads is either denied or negated at another place. And without resolving the conflict among the statements of the Upaniṣads, and harmonizing them it is not possible to develop a meaningful and coherent system of philosophy based on the Upaniṣads. Therefore, the first and foremost task in developing a philosophy of the Upaniṣads is to reconcile and harmonize the mutually conflicting Upaniṣadic statements. Thus, every philosopher of Vedānta has realized that to develop a meaningful and coherent system of philosophy based on the Upaniṣads it is essential to reconcile and harmonize the various Upaniṣadic texts and statements. According to Bādarāyaṇa, the first person to develop a systematic philosophy of Vedānta, either to understand the meaning of the Upaniṣads or to develop a philosophy based on them it is essential to reconcile (*samanvaya*) the various statements of the Upaniṣads.

Several problems of philosophic nature and worth, such as the existence and nature of *Brahman*, the reality of *ātman*, and the nature of its relationship with *Brahman*, the origin and nature of the phenomenal reality or the world of empirical experience, and the way it is related to *Brahman* are raised and discussed in the Upaniṣads. However, we do not find in the Upaniṣads any definite and conclusive statement or view on these problems. Different views on all the basic problems are freely expressed and discussed in the Upaniṣads, and the Upaniṣads have not endorsed any view or opinion. The various views expressed in the Upaniṣads, either on the nature of *Brahman*, or on the reality and nature of *ātman*, or about the origin and nature of the phenomenal reality are not consistent with each other. There is even conflict among them. Although each problem raised and discussed in the Upaniṣads is significant in its own way, the problem which is more basic or fundamental, and can throw light on or help in understanding other problems is the problem of the relationship between *Brahman* and the world of empirical experience. In other words, the real conflict we find among the statements of the Upaniṣads is regarding the origin and nature of the phenomenal reality or the world of empirical experience and the way it is related to *Brahman* or what is ultimately and objectively real. The problem has attracted the attention of almost all the philosophers of Vedānta who have discussed it extensively and comprehensively. And it is in terms of their approach to and understanding of the problem that different schools of Vedānta have come into existence. In their attempts to understand and resolve the problem of reconciliation different philosophers of Vedānta have tried to interpret the reality of the world of empirical experience and the nature and meaning of *Brahman* in their own characteristic ways. While some of them, like Śaṅkara, have tried to understand the meaning of the Upaniṣads in terms of the logic internal to them, some others, like Rāmānuja, have been influenced or inspired by religious ideas and beliefs which are not, strictly speaking, Upaniṣadic in origin, and are not compatible with the world-view of the Upaniṣads.

Another important thing which is relevant and significant in understanding the problem of reconciliation is what one thinks of the basic vision or the world-view of the Upaniṣads. Every interpreter or philosopher of the Upaniṣads has his own view or understanding of the vision or world-view of the Upaniṣads which he tries to support and justify on the basis of some of the Upaniṣadic statements and their interpretation. And if what some of the Upaniṣadic statements express is to be the basis as well as the authority for understanding the meaning of the Upaniṣads then there can be different interpretations of Vedānta, and all can be true to the Upaniṣads, or conversely every interpretation of Vedānta can be criticized and rejected on the basis of some of the Upaniṣadic statements as the Upaniṣads express different and even conflicting views on all important problems. It may, therefore, appear that the Upaniṣads are the source as well as the justification for different schools of Vedānta, for they all can find authority or justification in the Upaniṣads. In such a situation it is difficult to understand and judge which school of Vedānta is true to the Upaniṣads, or represents the philosophy of the Upaniṣads. Can we then say that the Upaniṣads are equally a source of inspiration and authority for different schools of Vedānta?

To understand the problem we have to discuss whether the Upaniṣads represent something in common. Do they have a vision or world-view despite the fact that they express different views on most of the basic problems? Do they have a common object or purpose? How are they related to the Veda, or what is their place of importance in the Śruti tradition? Can we say that they stand for certain theological or metaphysical views and doctrines? Are the Upaniṣads metaphysical in character? In other words, what is the source of their thought or wisdom?

Now, if we think that the Upaniṣads have a common purport then how to understand the meaning and validity of those statements which are in conflict with each other. There are several Upaniṣadic statements which are not compatible with each other. And if the chief purpose or object of the Upaniṣads is to teach the nature of *Brahman*, as it reveals itself at the level of human reality or within the reality of man, how to understand and explain the meaning and purpose of the statements which express different and mutually conflicting views on certain metaphysical and cosmological problems? On the other hand, if we think that the Upaniṣads represent or teach certain ideas or doctrines on some of the basic metaphysical problems, like the nature of *Brahman*, the origin of the world, etc. how to understand and explain the place and significance of certain statements which are descriptive in nature, and describe, for instance, the nature of human reality (*ātman*) or the nature of *Brahman* as it reveals itself within the reality of man? Can we then say that the Upaniṣads have no focus or vision, but express different views on various problems which are not, however, compatible with each other? How to approach the problem? Is reason sufficient to understand the problem of reconciliation? If the Upaniṣads, as an integral part of the Veda, are a continuation of Vedic revelation, though at a different level, can reason understand and resolve the problem of reconciliation?

Another basic problem in understanding the meaning of the Upaniṣads is how to understand the relationship between the language of the Upaniṣads and the vision or truth they try to express or communicate. In what sense the Upaniṣadic statements convey the vision or world-view of the Upaniṣads? Can they be literally true or is it sufficient to understand the meaning of the Upaniṣadic statements literally or in a straightforward manner? Can we understand the meaning of the Upaniṣadic statements without comprehending the vision or world-view of the Upaniṣads? In other words, we have to understand whether the statements of the Upaniṣads can convey their meaning individually or independently of other statements and texts.

Another important thing we have to keep in mind in understanding the meaning of the Upaniṣads is that they are primarily intended to teach or instruct the nature of *Brahman* as it reveals itself at the level of human reality (*adhyātma*) or within the reality of man. While the other Vedic texts, like the Saṁhitās and Brāhmaṇas, reveal the nature of the divine at the levels of deities and nature, the Upaniṣads reveal the nature of the divine at the level of human reality. When the Upaniṣads talk of *Brahman* they refer to the reality which is known directly and immediately, and is present within all, but not about a metaphysical reality which is postulated to explain the existence of the world. *Brahman* of the Upaniṣads cannot be equated with the notion of ultimate reality of speculative metaphysics. Although the Upaniṣads speak of *Brahman* which is direct and immediate the *Brahman*-experience which is direct and immediate is not described in the Upaniṣads. However, the Upaniṣadic statements on *Brahman* gain their meaning and authority in terms of the Vedic revelation expressed in the Vedic Saṁhitās, according to which, the divine or *Brahman* is known directly in the state of divine inspiration. The cardinal Upaniṣadic statements like "I am *Brahman*," "you are that," "consciousness or knowledge is *Brahman*" which are concerned with the reality of man gain their meaning and validity in terms of the Vedic revelation expressed in the Saṁhitās. And the Upaniṣadic concern with the reality of man (*ātman*) is mainly because of its capacity to reveal the nature of *Brahman* directly and immediately. When the Upaniṣads speak of *ātman* or self they speak of it as the revelation of *Brahman* at the human level. The Upaniṣadic concern for the knowledge of *ātman* is because of its capacity to reveal the nature of *Brahman* clearly and directly. Thus, most of the major Upaniṣadic statements depend on Vedic revelation contained in the Saṁhitās for their meaning and validity. And in this sense we can say that the Upaniṣads express succinctly the essence or meaning of Vedic revelation, besides revealing the nature of *Brahman* as it reveals itself at the level of human reality. What the Upaniṣads teach is, therefore, meaningful and intelligible only in relation to the Vedic revelation contained in the Saṁhitās. In other words, to comprehend the meaning of the Upaniṣads they are to be viewed and understood in relation to other Śruti texts.

These are some of the important problems which one has to consider before one tries to understand the meaning of the Upaniṣads or interpret them. However, not all the interpreters of the Upaniṣads have paid sufficient attention to these problems. And for most of the interpreters of Vedānta the Upaniṣads, as an integral part of Śruti tradition, seem to provide authority and justification for various sectarian religious beliefs and doctrines. They have tried to derive the sanctity and authority of the Upaniṣads to support and justify some of the sectarian religious beliefs and doctrines. In other words, instead of trying to understand the Upaniṣads philosophically they have tried to adapt them to serve the theological needs of sectarian religious traditions. Now, it is a different problem whether the Upaniṣads are basically religious in character or can, at least, lend support to certain religious beliefs and doctrines. If they are really religious in character the Upaniṣads would not have recognized the value of freedom of inquiry in understanding the truth. They are not dogmatic in their approach to any problem. We find in the Upaniṣads different and even conflicting views on all important problems, and no attempt is made in the Upaniṣads either to endorse or reject some of the views presented. In a sense, there is no accepted or official view in the Upaniṣads. All this is significant as the main purpose or object of the Upaniṣads is to teach or instruct the nature of *Brahman* as it reveals itself at the level of human reality, or within the reality of man. And to make the instruction effective the Upaniṣads have invented or adopted several methods and literary devices keeping in view the nature of the problem and the level of the taught. The famous dialogues of the Upaniṣads are intended to serve the purpose of teaching. Their purpose is pedagogic. We cannot, therefore, say that all the Upaniṣadic statements enjoy the same kind of authority and validity. Therefore, there can be no justification for employing the same method in trying to understand the meaning of all the Upaniṣadic statements. And all the Upaniṣadic statements cannot be adduced in support or justification of any metaphysical or theological view or doctrine.

Furthermore, what is basic to Śruti tradition, and distinguishes it from a religious tradition is the belief or view that truth is self-evident, or the divine is self-revealing. In the ultimate analysis, the divine or *Brahman* does not depend for its knowledge on the means of knowledge, including the Veda. *Brahman*, by its very nature, is eternally self-revealing, and therefore anyone who wants to know it can know it, or anyone who wants to see it can see it. It is present within all that we see and know, and is present within man as his true being or self (*ātman*). Thus the object of the Upaniṣads is not to reveal or make us know something which is otherwise unknown to us, but to reveal directly and perfectly the nature of what is known to all. In other words, the Upaniṣads are a source of knowledge of *Brahman* or *ātman* in the sense that they reveal the nature of *Brahman* or *ātman* truly and perfectly. The Upaniṣads are revelation in the sense that they reveal the nature of *Brahman* or the divine as it reveals itself at the level of human reality (*adhyātma*), or within the reality of man. And man is never devoid of self-knowledge or knowledge of himself. However, because of various subjective factors man fails to know or realize the true or objective nature of himself.

It is, therefore, the purpose of the Upaniṣads to guide and help man in knowing or realizing the true or objective nature of himself. Therefore, the significance and validity of the Upaniṣadic statements lie in their efficiency or efficacy to make one realize the truth for himself directly. The Upaniṣadic parable of the person from Gāndhāra who has lost his way home helps us in understanding the role or function of the Upaniṣads or the teacher in knowing the truth. A person from Gāndhāra was taken away from his country blindfolded, and was left in a far off place. However, the person could return to his place by inquiring from people about it because it is his place, and is already known to him.

Nevertheless, we find in the Upaniṣads different views on various philosophical or rather metaphysical problems, like the origin of the world, the nature of *Brahman*, the nature of *ātman* and the way the world and *ātman* are related to *Brahman*. And if we regard those views as representing the wisdom of the Upaniṣads or as revealed by the Upaniṣads we may be able to support or justify several metaphysical or theological views or doctrines either about *Brahman* or *ātman* or about the origin of the world. And different systems of metaphysics or theology have been developed on the basis of such statements. But the problem is how to understand and judge the validity of such systems or doctrines? What kind of validity do they enjoy? Can they have the status and authority of revelation? Can they be really justified or supported on the basis of the Upaniṣads? However, one important thing about such doctrines or systems is that they are not developed solely or completely on the basis of the Upaniṣads, as in their development rational understanding of man plays a significant role. In trying to develop a coherent system of philosophy on the basis of the Upaniṣads they are interpreted. And unless the Upaniṣadic statements are coordinated and reconciled the meaning or the philosophy of the Upaniṣads cannot be comprehended. And in doing so if one presupposes that the Upaniṣads represent certain beliefs or doctrines on some of the basic metaphysical or cosmological problems the purpose of interpretation will be to develop a coherent system of metaphysics or theology. On the other hand, if one regards that the real purpose of the Upaniṣads is to awaken man to the reality of the divine that is present within himself then the purpose of interpretation will be completely different. However, even if one thinks that the Upaniṣads represent certain metaphysical or theological views one should be open- minded and non-dogmatic in his understanding of the meaning of the Upaniṣads as the Upaniṣads are basically non-dogmatic in their approach. No deterministic thought or philosophy can truly represent the thought or wisdom of the Upaniṣads. More importantly, the Upaniṣads are known for their insights into the nature of human reality. They are revelation of the divine at the human level, and this should not be lost sight of while developing the philosophy of the Upaniṣads. However, some of the interpreters of the Vedānta think that the Upaniṣads stand for certain metaphysical doctrines or ideas, and therefore the object of interpretation, according to them, is to present the doctrines in a proper perspective. They think that the object of the Upaniṣads is to reveal the nature of *Brahman*, the ultimate source and explanation of the world, and as part of Śruti the Upaniṣads are a source of authority on all important metaphysical problems. They, therefore, give more importance to those statements of the Upaniṣads which seem to be more positive and even definite about the nature of *Brahman*, the origin of the world, etc. than those statements in which the Upaniṣads deny ultimate and objective validity to such statements.

Now, it is difficult to compare and judge the validity of different schools or systems of philosophy based on the Upaniṣads, as they all are based on or are inspired by the Upaniṣads, and seem to represent them. The Upaniṣadic authority and justification can be shown in favour or support of each system or school. However, one's approach to and understanding of the Upaniṣads depend upon what one regards as the basic vision or world-view of the Upaniṣads.

Depending upon what one thinks is the world-view of the Upaniṣads one tries to interpret the Upaniṣadic statements. If one thinks that *Brahman* of the Upaniṣads is something given, and is to be realized directly as one's true being (*ātman*) his approach to understanding the meaning of the Upaniṣads will be significantly different from that of the one who sees *Brahman* as a metaphysical idea or principle meant to explain the origin and existence of the world. However, in any attempt to understand the concepts and relate them with a view to developing a system of metaphysics around them it is essential to follow the logic internal to the concepts. For instance, when it is said in the Upaniṣads that *Brahman* after creating the world entered into it to the last detail we may try to understand and explain the process of creation and the manner and meaning of *Brahman* entering into the creation. And if such statements are taken to represent the Upaniṣadic doctrine of creation instead of expressing the world-view of the Upaniṣads one has to philosophically analyse and understand the concepts involved, and the possible ways in which they could logically be related. This involves rational understanding of the concepts, and the ways in which they can be related. But as there are several statements in the Upaniṣads expressing different and even conflicting views on all the basic problems there can be no one or deterministic way of understanding the nature and meaning of the concepts involved. They can be defined and related in different ways depending upon one's commitment to a world-view. However, some of the interpreters of Vedānta are interested more in adapting Vedānta to serve the sectarian theological needs than in understanding the meaning or philosophy of the Upaniṣads. They do not try to see or understand the logical possibilities of a concept, or extend the process of logical development of a concept to its logical end. If one starts the process of logical development of a concept, either individually or in relation to other concepts, the process should not be stopped at a point or stage which is convenient or acceptable either to himself or to the system. But this is not, however, the case with those who are interested in justifying or supporting a system of metaphysics or theology on the authority of the Upaniṣads. For instance, to attribute any form of causation to *Brahman*, in the process of explaining the existence of the world in terms of *Brahman*, is to deny *Brahman* its absolute character and perfection as causation in any form is not compatible with the absolute perfection of *Brahman*. Moreover, the process of logical analysis of a concept may lead to skepticism, or even to nihilism as the Mahāyāna Buddhists have tried to show. Thus, when one comes to realize, in the process of developing a concept logically, that it is not possible to defend or justify a system of metaphysics or theology in terms of the logical analysis and development of concepts one tries to evoke the authority of revelation (Upaniṣads) forgetting the fact that the process of development is logical, and is, therefore, bound by the rules of logic. Therefore one should not either start the process of logical analysis and development of the concepts or should not stop the process at a point or stage convenient either to himself or to the system, as in that case the whole process of developing a system of metaphysics on the basis of some of the Upaniṣadic statements proves itself futile. And even when it is developed it will not have the validity of either revelation or of reason. Moreover, we have to remember that *Brahman* or *ātman* which the Upaniṣads speak of is not a metaphysical principle or idea, but something that is directly and immediately experienced, and is objectively real. Although we try to conceptualize such an experience or vision the doctrines and the systems built in terms of them cannot adequately or truly represent or express the experience and its meaning. In other words, what transcends the concepts cannot be judged in terms of the logic of concepts. The meaning and validity of what transcends the categories of empirical experience and understanding cannot be grasped and judged in terms of such categories. And to try to make *Brahman* meaningful in terms of categories of empirical understanding is to make *Brahman* a part of empirical reality.

A major problem faced by almost all the interpreters of the Upaniṣads or the philosophers of Vedānta is how to reconcile and harmonize the two kinds of statements found in the Upaniṣads. They are not compatible with each other as what is stated positively in one kind of statements is not regarded as ultimately or objectively real in the other kind of statements. Such statements are mostly about the reality of the world of empirical experience and the manner in which it is related to *Brahman*, an objectively existing reality. In other words, the problem is how to reconcile the reality of *Brahman* with that of the world. The problem can be formulated differently. If what Śruti reveals is ultimately and objectively real, and is significantly different from what our empirical experience reveals, though both refer to the same reality, how to explain and reconcile both the accounts of what is there. In other words, how to reconcile the reality of *Brahman* which the Upaniṣads reveal with that of the world which is given to our empirical experience and understanding. Although we find in the Upaniṣads different views about the relationship between *Brahman* and the word no view can be taken as the view of the Upaniṣads, for the Upaniṣads do not endorse any view. Different views on all important philosophical problems are freely expressed in the Upaniṣads, and we have no justification for accepting them all as true to the Upaniṣads. They are expressed mostly by way of teaching the nature of *Brahman*. And if we accept the world-view of the Upaniṣads we should not try to reconcile the statements as they do not belong to the same level, and do not have the same kind of authority and validity. They do not have the same logic, or are not amenable to the same logic. What is transcendentally meaningful and valid may not be so from an empirical point of view, and vice versa.

However, this problem has attracted the attention of all the Vedāntins, and they have followed or adopted different approaches to understand and resolve the problem. In the history of the philosophical development of Vedānta we find several ways of reconciling the two kinds of the Upaniṣadic statements or reconciling the reality of *Brahman* with that of the world. Each attempt is significant in its own way, and together have contributed to the philosophical growth or development of Vedānta, and its richness. Although there are several other problems which are philosophically significant, and are discussed by almost all the Vedāntins we have chosen for discussion the more basic problem of reconciliation between *Brahman* and the world, or the absolute and the phenomenal.

We have taken for philosophical discussion some of the major thinkers who are known for their approaches to the problem. They all have tried to understand and resolve the problem in their own characteristic ways. However, keeping in view the importance of the problem and different approaches adopted by different thinkers I have named the chapters after the thinkers who are representative of such approaches. Therefore, I have named the chapter on Kashmir Śaivism as Abhinavagupta, a representative thinker of that school. And in all the chapters I have limited my discussion to the problem of reconciliation between the two kinds of Vedānta statements or between the reality *Brahman* and that of the world as approached by different thinkers. Each approach to the problem is significant, and the way the problem is sought to be resolved by different Vedāntins has helped in understanding the complexity of the problem, or the different dimensions of it. Each approach may be meaningful and satisfying in terms of one's religious faith and commitment, but the purpose of discussion in this work is to understand and evaluate the problem philosophically as almost all the thinkers chosen for discussion are pre-eminently philosophical in their approaches and understanding. The problem is philosophical, and so is my treatment of it throughout the work. All the thinkers are great in their own ways, and no attempt is made to compare them. I have tried to present and discuss their general philosophical positions as far as that is relevant in understanding the problem of reconciliation, and tried to see how each approach has added a new dimension to the problem. The object of this work is to project the philosophical development of Vedānta from the Upaniṣads to Sri Aurobindo, and to be comprehensive and meaningful the discussion is confined to one major problem of Vedānta which has attracted the attention of almost all the Vedāntins. And almost all of them have tried to understand and resolve the problem philosophically. However, keeping in view the significance of the problem, and for the sake of projecting its problematic character, I have confined the discussion to the problem itself, and have not tried to present the general thought of the thinkers discussed.

2

Upaniṣads

OUR understanding of the Upaniṣads depends largely upon our attitude towards the Veda, and its relation to the Upaniṣads. Although we study the Upaniṣads, and try to comprehend their meaning independently of other Śruti texts we should not be oblivious to the fact that the Upaniṣads are an integral part of the Veda or Śruti tradition. The Upaniṣads not only form part of the Veda but also depend upon it for their meaning and authority. Even though Śruti consists of several texts, such as the Saṁhitās, Brāhmaṇas, Āranyakas and the Upaniṣads, it is one and integral as all the texts of Śruti try to express the same world-view or vision, though in their own characteristic ways. The world-view which is reflected and expressed commonly in all the texts of Śruti forms the basis of their unity. Otherwise, the various texts of Śruti will have only an external or formal unity as a collection of texts classed together and termed as Śruti with no internal cohesion and unity of meaning. All the Vedic texts are handed over from generation to generation by an oral tradition (Śruti), and therefore belong to a genre of literature known as Śruti.

According to the modern understanding of the Śruti tradition, which includes both the Veda and Vedānta, Vedānta contains more evolved and philosophically enlightened thought when compared to the other texts of the Veda. However, according to the traditional view or understanding, the Upaniṣads express the same vision or world-view which is common to all the texts of the Veda. The object of the Upaniṣads is to reveal the divine and its nature, which the Vedic Sahṁitās reveal, though at a different level. On the other hand, it is only when we think that Śruti, like any other literature, is a product of human creativity and understanding we can think in terms of evolution of its thought, and grade or class it accordingly as primitive or developed or evolved. Accordingly, we may regard the thought or wisdom reflected in the Vedic Saṁhitās and other Śruti literature as primitive in comparison to the thought or wisdom reflected in the Upaniṣads. The thought or wisdom expressed in the Upaniṣads is more evolved and philosophic. In other words, the Upaniṣads are the culmination of a thought process which had its beginning in the Vedic Saṁhitās. The Saṁhitās are poetic, mythological and even anthropomorphic, and are concerned more with the manifestation of the divine than with the divine in itself. They mark the beginning of a thought process of which the Upaniṣads are the culmination. Thus, it may be said that while in the Vedic Saṁhitās we find the beginnings of Indian mind trying to grasp the nature and meaning of the divine, in the Upaniṣads it has attained a level of abstraction, objectivity and subtlety. The Upaniṣads are more conceptual and philosophic in understanding the problems with which the Vedic seers are also concerned.

To view the Upaniṣadic thought as a development and culmination of Vedic thought is to regard the Veda as a result of human enquiry and understanding. If we regard the Veda consisting of the Saṁhitās, Brāhmaṇas, Āraṇyakas and the Upaniṣads as a result of human understanding and wisdom then our approach to understand its meaning in a developmental or evolutionary perspective would be perfectly justified. We may then be justified in thinking that the Saṁhitās represent the groping of human mind into the mysteries of nature, while in the Upaniṣads it has attained a level of philosophic understanding and maturity. This kind of approach to understand the Veda and its meaning has led to the creation of a gulf or a gap between the Veda and the Upaniṣads or Vedānta. While in the past a distinction is made, and antagonism created between the two schools of Vedic interpretation, namely, Pūrva-Mīmāṁsā and Uttara-Mīmāṁsā, in terms of ritualism and wisdom, in modern times a gulf is created between the Veda and Vedānta in terms of primitive and developed or evolved thought. The gulf between the two interpretations of the Veda, or the two schools of Mīmāṁsā, is due mainly to the prominence or importance given either to the Brāhmaṇas (liturgical texts of the Veda) or to the Upaniṣads in interpreting the Veda. The basic concern of the traditional Indian interpreters of the Veda in general, and the two Mīmāṁsās in particular, is not so much to understand the source of the wisdom expressed in the Veda, and its meaning but to adapt it to practical religious needs of people. The Pūrva-Mīmāṁsā which is an attempt to defend and justify the ritualistic aspect of the Vedic religion relied largely, if not wholly, on the Brāhmaṇa texts of the Veda to support and justify its position. Some of the Vedic hymns are employed or utilized in all the Vedic rituals in so far as they are regarded as relevant in their performance. Brāhmaṇa texts contain detailed instructions about the procedure involved in the performance of various Vedic rites and rituals, and their justification. And the justification is meaningful in terms of Vedic ontology or world-view. It is only in the light of the Vedic world-view the various Vedic rites and rituals gain their significance and meaning.

It is an undeniable fact that the Veda or the Śruti tradition is the primary source of Hinduism, especially in its classical form. Veda is also a source of a major philosophical tradition of India. However, as the Veda is not primarily a philosophical or metaphysical tradition we cannot say that the Upaniṣads are its culmination. The Veda never says that it represents the wisdom of man. No Vedic seer has claimed to himself the source of wisdom expressed in the Veda.[1] The Vedic hymns

1. What is commonly prayed for by the seers of the *Ṛgveda* is the gift of divine inspiration, the source of Vedic wisdom expressed through the hymns of the Veda. The truth that is expressed through the hymns of the Veda is not due to the effort and wisdom of the seers. They have not said anywhere in the Veda →

are not created to express the wisdom of the Vedic seers. They are due to divine inspiration, or express the wisdom born of divine inspiration. The source of wisdom expressed through the hymns of the Veda is divine inspiration. As this aspect of the Vedic wisdom is clearly and definitely stated in the Veda we have no reason to think that the Veda represents or expresses human wisdom, or the wisdom of the Vedic seers. On the other hand, if the Veda is only an articulation and expression of human wisdom we will be perfectly justified in trying to understand its meaning in terms of the categories of human understanding. We can then also think of the development or evolution of Vedic thought from the Saṁhitās to the Upaniṣads.

Nevertheless, we find in the Vedic Saṁhitās a clear evidence of human speculation on some of the metaphysical problems, or more specifically the problems of ontology. Nāsadīya-Sūkta of the *Ṛgveda* expresses human speculation or understanding on some of the fundamental problems of ontology. And we also find as early as the *Ṛgveda* clear signs of skepticism in such matters. "Who knows, who can tell us the origins of the world. Not even gods can tell us for they come into existence after the creation of the world."[2] In the *Ṛgveda* almost all the speculative hymns end in skepticism. This, however, is not the case with most of the hymns which represent or express the world-view of the Veda. They are not speculative in character. They are essentially prayers and praises, and express the deep sense of devotion to the divine though they are addressed to various deities either individually or collectively. They express the devotion that is

→ that the hymns express their understanding and wisdom. Divine inspiration, the source of Vedic wisdom, is a divine gift which the seers of the Veda wish to return in gratitude to the divine by means of prayer, just as a shepherd returns the sheep to the master. It is only the literary form of the hymn or the language and metaphors used in creating a hymn that reflect the creativity of the seers. See *Ṛgveda*, 1.114.9, 10.72.3, 5.48.5.

2. *Ṛgveda*, 10.72.2-3, 5.48.5 (*na tasya vidma puruṣtvatavyam*).

divinely inspired, and the seers of the Veda proclaim unequivocally that the divinely inspired devotion is the source of the wisdom expressed through the hymns of the Veda.[3] In other words, when the divinely inspired devotion is expressed in language the hymns of the Veda are born. Therefore there can be no justification for regarding the Veda, especially the Saṁhitās, as reflecting or representing the wisdom of man, either speculative or intuitive, on certain theological or philosophical problems like the nature of the divine, and the manner of its manifestation. Divinely inspired devotion is seen as an end in itself, as in experiencing it the seers have realized the ultimate fulfilment of their lives. Devotion (brahma) is not regarded by the seers of the Veda as a means for attaining anything else. It is an end in itself, and those who have experienced it are known as seers (*ṛsi*) and seer-poets (*kavi*). *Brahman* in its original or Vedic usage as brahma means the divinely inspired devotion, and by extension prayer as well as the hymns that express prayer.[4]

If the Veda consists primarily of prayers and praises addressed to various deities, either individually or collectively, in what sense we can think of it as having anything to do with theology or even philosophy. The speculative hymns of the Veda, which are a few in number, are generally skeptical about metaphysical problems. However, they do not go against the spirit of the Veda as they speculate mainly about the nature of ultimate reality or the divine in itself. As most

3. The seers of the Veda say that they sing the devotion that is divinely inspired (*devatvaṁ brahma gāyata*) *ṚV*, 8.32.27. Only the literary form of the hymns is the creation of the seers, but not the truth or wisdom that is expressed through the hymns.

4. In its Vedic usage *brahma* primarily means divinely inspired devotion, and by extension prayer as well as the hymns that express prayer. *Ṛgveda* is a book of prayers as the word *ṛk* means worship (*arca*). And the primary means of Vedic worship of the divine is to pray in reverence and to bow down (*namaḥ*) before the divine. Bowing down in reverence expresses the state of divinely inspired devotion. See the *Central Philosophy* of the *Ṛgveda* by the same author.

of the Vedic hymns are prayers and praises addressed to the deities they are essential to understanding the meaning of the Veda. They are created to articulate and express the divinely inspired devotion. And as the nature in its diverse phenomena is the immediate source of divine inspiration to the seers of the Veda, the nature is seen as a manifestation or an abode of the divine. As each phenomenon of nature is the immediate source of inspiration of the divine to the seers each phenomenon is seen as the dwelling place or an abode of a deity. Therefore, the real source of knowledge of the divine to the seers of the Veda is divine inspiration. The seers of the Veda proclaim that they have come to know the divine not because of their own ability and effort, but because of divine inspiration.[5] They see nature as a manifestation of the divine because of divine inspiration of which nature is the immediate source. This is expressed in poetic language of the Veda by addressing each phenomenon of nature as a deity or as a manifestation of the divine. In praising the deities, either individually or collectively, the seers have tried to describe the divine and its nature, or the divine qualities which all the deities share in common. The hymns also describe the deities in their phenomenal aspect in which each deity is distinct from other deities, as in their phenomenal character each deity possesses the qualities of a natural phenomenon which it represents. Therefore, in the Veda each deity is addressed and praised in terms of both divine and phenomenal attributes or qualities. While the divine qualities are attributed commonly to all the deities, the qualities that belong to nature are not attributed commonly to all the deities. The qualities of a phenomenon of nature are attributed to the deity which represents it or in which the deity dwells. Therefore, nature in its diverse phenomena is addressed and praised not because of its phenomenal qualities and splendour but because of its being a manifestation of the divine. Each phenomenon of nature is thus seen as an abode of a deity. For instance, Agni is not

---

5. *na tasya vidma puruṣtvatavyam* — *Ṛ̥V*, 5.48.5.

simple fire, it is something more, it is divine, and that is revealed to the seers in the state of divine inspiration. Therefore, Agni as a manifestation of the divine is an object of worship and prayer. Thus, the chief object of the Veda is to reveal the divine as it manifests itself in and through nature, or to reveal the divine dimension or aspect of nature.

What is the nature of the divine in itself is a matter of logical or speculative understanding. When the presence of the divine is experienced in nature one may try to understand the nature of the divine as such or in itself as well as the manner or mode of its manifestation in nature, or the relationship between the divine and the deities. This kind of problems though attracted the attention of the Vedic seers they are given secondary importance. However, they form the prime concern of some of the Āraṇyakas and the Upaniṣads. The problem whether the divine that is experienced directly by the seers of the Veda due to divine inspiration can be of any significance and value in understanding the nature of the divine in itself as well as the mode or manner of its manifestation in nature has also attracted the attention of various Indian philosophers. Thus, if there is any persistent problem or a problem that is being continuously discussed both in the Vedic and Vedānta traditions it is not about the existence of the divine but about its nature and the nature of its relationship to the world of empirical experience. If we find some significant philosophical development in the tradition of Vedānta it is with regard to the problem of relationship between the divine and the world of empirical experience, or the relationship between the numinous and phenomenal. It is the problem which has exercised the minds of almost all the thinkers and interpreters of Vedānta.

As the Upaniṣads belong to the Veda integrally they are revelatory in character. They form part of Vedic revelation. However, we find in the Upaniṣads a clear and definite assertion of the importance of human enquiry and understanding in knowing the truth. This is evident in almost all the Upaniṣads, and more so in all the major and earlier

Upaniṣads. In all the well-known Upaniṣadic dialogues, as between Yājñyavalka and Janaka, Āruṇi and Śvetaketu, Naciketā and Yama, the spirit of inquiry is given importance, and the need to discuss and understand the problems related to truth is recognized. The human right to know the truth cannot be thwarted even by the gods as the *Bṛhadāraṇyaka Upaniṣad* asserts.[6] One more important thing we find in the Upaniṣads is their basic concern for knowing or discovering the truth which is truly universal. More significantly, they try to provide justification, either rational or experiential, to what they teach. The Upaniṣads seldom make statements about truth which we are supposed to accept on their authority. The most significant statements they make about *Brahman* or *ātman*, the major concern of the Upaniṣads, assert that *Brahman* is the inner ruler of all, including man. Can we, therefore, say that the Upaniṣads are basically philosophical in their attitude and approach to the basic problems they discussed, and therefore rational understanding of man is sufficient to understand their meaning? And if we think that the Upaniṣads are the real beginning of Vedānta philosophy, and they are primarily philosophical in their attitude and approach we need not view them in relation to the Veda to understand their meaning. They can have meaning independently of the Veda or the Veda may not prove to be helpful in understanding the meaning and validity of Vedānta. Is it then the case that though traditionally Veda and Vedānta are viewed as integrally related they are in reality two independent traditions each having its own authority and validity? Can we, therefore, admit that to understand the Upaniṣads it is not essential to study and understand the Veda? Our understanding of the Veda may have only historical value and significance in understanding the Upaniṣads as we can then understand the evolution of Vedic thought which has reached its culmination in the Upaniṣads. The Upaniṣads are the culmination of the thought process which has its beginning in the Vedic Saṁhitās.

6. *Bṛhadāraṇyaka Upaniṣad*, 1.4.10.

Another major reason for viewing the Veda and Vedānta independently of each other, it may be pointed out, is the fact that the basic concern of most of the Upaniṣads is to analyse and understand the nature of *ātman* or the self of man. But even if we recognize the fact that the major concern of most of the Upaniṣads is the reality of man or *ātman* we cannot in terms of an empirical analysis and understanding reach the Upaniṣadic position or conclusion that *ātman* is *Brahman*, which is all. Empirical analysis and understanding of self may not prove helpful in understanding the significance of the basic Upaniṣadic statements about *ātman*, such as "I am *Brahman*," "*ātman* is *Brahman*," "you are That." The Buddhist analysis of self has led them to the view that it is non-substantial, or has no objective existence or reality. We shall soon discuss whether the Upaniṣads have attained the knowledge of self on the basis of ordinary analysis and understanding or they have tried to articulate and present in a philosophic way the truth about self based on revelation. Is it the case that the Upaniṣads try to communicate the truth that is directly and immediately known or realized in a language that is intelligible to rational understanding of man? The latter seems to be the real intention of the Upaniṣads, as the purpose of all the dialogues, and the subtle arguments they provide in support and justification of the truth they represent is primarily to teach or instruct the revealed truth, which is the literary meaning of the term Upaniṣad.

The Veda and Vedānta are integral to each other as without the Vedic revelation communicated through the hymns of the Veda what the Upaniṣads say or teach will have no basis in direct experience. Therefore, to regard the Upaniṣads as having authority and validity independently of the Veda is to undermine the revealed character and authority of the Upaniṣads. The truth they represent is not self-evident, and at the same time it is not intelligible purely in terms of man's rational understanding. The Upaniṣadic thought is not metaphysical in nature, and even when we admit that the Upaniṣads recognize the value of human inquiry and understanding they are to be based on and guided by what is directly experienced by the seers of the Veda. The Vedic revelation is the source of inspiration for the Upaniṣads, and their wisdom. They restate or represent in a philosophic way the truth revealed in the Vedic Saṁhitās. However, the Upaniṣads are known for two important things. They articulate and express in more and more clear terms the essence of the Veda, or the Vedic world-view. The term *upaniṣad* also means essence.[7] The Vedic world-view which is reflected in all the Śruti literature, including the Upaniṣads, is expressed in the Upaniṣads in a manner which is more meaningful and intelligible to human understanding as their main purpose is to teach the truth. The Upaniṣads are more philosophical, coherent and systematic when compared to other Vedic literature. Furthermore, the Upaniṣads are a continuation of the Vedic revelation in the sense that they reveal the nature of the divine at the human level (*adhyātma*). We have to remember in this connection the Vedic or Śruti classification of all that is there into three realms of *ādhidaivika*, *ādhibhautika* and *ādhyātmika*. The chief object of the Veda is to reveal the nature of the divine as it reveals itself at all the three levels or in all the three realms. The Vedic Saṁhitās which are the basic source of revelation of the divine and its nature, however, reveal the nature of the divine at the level of nature. The object of Vedic revelation as expressed in the Vedic Saṁhitās is to reveal the nature of the divine as it reveals itself in and through the diverse phenomena of nature. The Brāhmaṇas which are primarily liturgical texts try to see the divine within the physical realm which though may appear to be fanciful is nevertheless meaningful if we are in tune with the world-view of the Veda. If all that is there is a manifestation of the divine, and express its creative wisdom (*kāvya*) then trying to see the divine in all the varied forms of its manifestation is really meaningful. In all the Vedic rituals, which the Brāhmaṇas deal with, the various elements of nature are symbolically identified with

7. *Mahābhārata*, Śānti-Parva, 25.11-12; See also *BṛhUp*, 2.1.20.

the deities, and thus with the divine. The important or the primary Vedic ritual of *yajña* is itself a symbolic representation of the divine act of self-manifestation.

However, either in the Saṁhitās or in the Brāhmaṇas nothing significant is said about man, or no significant attempt is made to understand the phenomenon of man. Some of the Āraṇyaka texts are concerned with the phenomenon of man. It is only in the Upaniṣads a systematic attempt is made to analyse and understand comprehensively the reality of man so as to discover the divine within it, as well as to relate the divine in man with the divine revealed outside the reality of man. We cannot, however, say that only in the Upaniṣads an attempt is made to know or understand the nature of the divine in itself as well as in its relation to the world of manifestation. The Veda is nothing if it is not a revelation of the divine. It is the basic source of the Śruti view of the divine. Therefore, the Upaniṣads are not a fresh source of revelation of the divine but a continuation of the Vedic revelation though at a different level. While the Vedic Saṁhitās and Brāhmaṇas reveal the divine at the level of deities and nature, the Upaniṣads reveal the nature of the divine at the human level or within the reality of man. This in a sense explains why the Upaniṣads are more significant and meaningful to man than the other Vedic texts. They reveal the divine within the reality of man. However, the Vedic revelation of the divine is not complete without the Upaniṣads, as the divine manifests and reveals itself in all that is there, including man. Therefore, in trying to understand the meaning of the Upaniṣads we should not disassociate or separate them from the rest of Śruti literature or tradition though for the purpose of systematic and comprehensive study we may distinguish them from the rest of Śruti literature.

As the Upaniṣads form part of Vedic revelation or belong integrally to Śruti tradition a simple rational approach may not be adequate to understand them. Nevertheless, to an extent we have to depend on our rational analysis and understanding in understanding the Upaniṣads as the truth they represent is not altogether unknown to us. The Upaniṣads speak of *Brahman* or *ātman* that is present within all as their essence, and within man as his self, and therefore we know what the Upaniṣads speak about or refer to. It is directly accessible to man. Furthermore, the Upaniṣads speak of *Brahman* that is known directly and immediately, but not of a reality that is completely unknown to man. While rational understanding and analysis may help man in knowing the self as something more than his body and mind, its divine nature or dimension in which it is also the reality of all can be known through Śruti. The knowledge that *ātman* is not only the self of man but also the self or essence of all that is there is not possible through empirical analysis and rational understanding. It is the Veda which teaches that *ātman* or *Brahman* is the self of man as well as the self or essence of all. One's knowledge of oneself based on empirical analysis and understanding will not help him in realizing his oneness with *Brahman* and all. Therefore, what Śruti teaches about self is beyond the ordinary or rational understanding of man. The nature of self as taught in the Upaniṣads cannot be known without the help of the Upaniṣads. Otherwise, the Buddhist analysis of self may be adequate to know the nature of self. Empirical analysis and understanding of self, though is helpful in revealing the nature of self, cannot reveal the nature of self completely and perfectly as no empirical understanding of self is universally valid. Ordinary understanding of self leaves something about it unexplained, and it may lead to the view that the reality of self is an illusion or something subjective. On the other hand, the knowledge of self the Upaniṣads speak about is more than any empirical knowledge of it. Nevertheless, as the Upaniṣads do not speak about self which is otherwise unknown to man the Upaniṣadic knowledge of self differs from the empirical knowledge of it only in terms of completeness and perfection. Otherwise both refer to the same reality. The meaningfulness of the Upaniṣads to all, including non-Hindus, is mainly because of their basic concern with the reality of man, and their insights into its nature. They try to reveal the real or objective nature of man which they claim is universally valid.

II

Before we try to understand the philosophy of the Upaniṣads we have to discuss the following. Is there anything that is common to all the Upaniṣads, or is there any theme or doctrine that unites all the texts known as Upaniṣads? Is there any doctrine or theology that runs through and unites all the Upaniṣads? Do they aim at understanding and expounding a problem though they differ in their approaches to it? Is it the approach that is common to all the Upaniṣads? Do all the Upaniṣads follow or adopt the same method in understanding the problem of *Brahman* or *ātman*? Is their unity due to or based on their revealed character? All the texts known as Upaniṣads are so-called because they belong to the same genre of literature. They belong integrally to the Śruti tradition, and share the character of revelation. Is their unity due to a vision or world-view which they all share and express in common? Can we say that the Upaniṣads share in common a world-view or an ontological vision which runs commonly through all of them though apparently each Upaniṣad is concerned with understanding a specific problem? Is it the case that though the same world-view or vision is reflected in all the Upaniṣads it is articulated differently in different Upaniṣads as each Upaniṣad approaches it in its own creative way?

Attempts are made traditionally to understand the Upaniṣads as dealing mainly with the reality and nature of *Brahman*, and the way it is related to *ātman* understood as the reality or self of man. They are seen as concerned mainly with ontological problems though we find in them several other problems discussed. It may be said that the reality of *Brahman* is the ruling idea of the Upaniṣads, and therefore we may regard them as dealing with *brahma-vidyā*. While some of the Upaniṣads deal with the problem of *Brahman* in itself, some other Upaniṣads try to understand *Brahman* in relation to man and world. As the primary concern of the Upaniṣads is *Brahman* we may say that the Upaniṣads are united in the object of their enquiry, that is, *Brahman*. Therefore, many have tried to understand the meaning or philosophy of the Upaniṣads in terms of the concept of *Brahman,* and its development. Accordingly, many thinkers and interpreters of the Upaniṣads have tried to reconcile the various conceptions of *Brahman* as found in the Upaniṣads. In the process of developing the concept of *Brahman* they have also tried to understand its nature in relation to the world of empirical experience, or to reconcile the various theories or doctrines of creation as found in the Upaniṣads with *Brahman.* We find several theories or views on creation in the Upaniṣads, and all of them are not compatible with each other. So is the case with *Brahman*'s relationship with the reality of man. These problems, and the way they are viewed and discussed gave rise to different interpretations of the Upaniṣads, or to different schools of Vedānta. Interpreters of the Upaniṣads differ among themselves basically in terms of their understanding of the nature of *Brahman,* and the way it is related to the world of empirical experience, including man.

In their attempts to understand the Upaniṣadic concept of *Brahman* the various interpreters of Vedānta faced a common problem of how to reconcile and harmonize different Upaniṣadic statements either on *Brahman* or on the nature of the world and its relation to *Brahman.* The various interpretations are significant in terms of their attempts to reconcile and harmonize the various Upaniṣadic statements or views on *Brahman,* and the manner in which it is related to the world of empirical experience. If all the Upaniṣads are unanimous about the nature and meaning of *Brahman,* and define it in the same way or language there would have been no problem of developing a coherent doctrine of *Brahman,* and consequently there would have been no different interpretations of Vedānta. I am not going to discuss here the different views about the nature of *Brahman* as interpreted by different schools of Vedānta, or by different interpreters of the Upaniṣads. But we can point out what is common to all the interpretations. What is common to all the interpretations or what is commonly presupposed by all the Vedantins in developing different doctrines about *Brahman* is that the Upaniṣads are amenable to a systematic and coherent interpretation. And if the Upaniṣads are really amenable to a systematic and coherent interpretation we have to admit that they are rationally intelligible. And if they are rationally intelligible different Upaniṣadic statements, either about *Brahman* or about the world, cannot have the same kind of authority and validity as they not only agree among themselves but even contradict each other. In such a situation it will be a major problem to decide which of the Upaniṣadic statements are to be taken as more valid and authoritative. On the other hand, if we accept that the authority of the Upaniṣads is that of revelation (Śruti) then all the Upaniṣadic statements are to be regarded as equally valid and authoritative. But in that case the authority of Śruti becomes dubious. Thus, in the face of mutually conflicting statements on any problem one's approach to the Upaniṣads depends upon one's attitude to the Upaniṣads as well as one's understanding of the meaning of revelation (Śruti).

In their attempts to prove or justify the validity of their interpretation different interpreters of the Upaniṣads have tried to rely upon certain Upaniṣadic statements, and ignore or play down the importance of other statements. While some of the Upaniṣadic statements are taken to be literally true and meaningful others which do not agree with their understanding or interpretation of the Upaniṣads are regarded as metaphorical in their meaning, and hence secondary in their importance and validity. Considering such attempts we may not be able to say that the unity of the Upaniṣads does not consist in certain doctrines purported to be central to the Upaniṣads, like that of *Brahman* or *ātman*, and the way it is related to the world. Therefore, it is a crucial problem whether a consistent and coherent doctrine or theology can be constructed taking into consideration all the Upaniṣadic statements as all the statements are equally valid and significant from the point of view of the Upaniṣads. One's approach to and understanding of the problem depends largely upon what one regards as the main purpose or object of the Upaniṣads, or on what one thinks is the world-view of the Upaniṣads. It involves a comprehensive view or understanding of the Upaniṣads.

In almost all the Upaniṣads *Brahman* is known or is indicated as the internal ruler or the self of man. In the major Upaniṣads, like the *Bṛhadāraṇyaka, Chāndogya* and *Kaṭha, Brahman* is known as the *ātman* in man. This is the major thrust of almost all the Upaniṣads. *Ātman* in man is identified with *Brahman,* the reality of all that is there. Can we, therefore, say that the Upaniṣadic approach to *Brahman* is through an analysis and understanding of human reality or human self? Is it the case that the starting point of *Brahman* enquiry in Upaniṣads is man rather than the world as we find it in other Śruti literature? The Upaniṣads start with the reality of man, and come to know *Brahman* as the *ātman* of man. In this context it is crucial to understand whether the Upaniṣadic seers knowing what *Brahman* is tried to find it out within the reality of man, or have they come to know *Brahman* while understanding the reality of man. Now, we have to admit that the seers of the Upaniṣads knowing what *Brahman* is tried to discover or realize its presence and nature within the reality of man. Otherwise, we have to explain the reasons or justification for identifying the *ātman* of man with *Brahman,* the ultimate reality or the reality of all that is there. However, we do not come across in the Upaniṣads any reasons or justification for doing so as the seers of the Upaniṣads have not tried to provide any justification for identifying *ātman* with *Brahman.* While in the Vedic Saṁhitās *Brahman* or the divine is known as it reveals itself in and through the phenomena of nature, in the Upaniṣads it is known as it reveals itself within the reality of man. Therefore, seeing *Brahman* within the reality of man does not mean seeing it as the reality of man. To say that *Brahman* is the reality of man because it is the reality of all is significantly different from saying that *Brahman* is all because it is the reality or self of man. We cannot say that *Brahman* is the reality of all because it is the self of man as it lacks any kind of justification. There is no link, either logical or experiential, between the self of man and all that is. However, it presupposes the idea that what is there within man is also there within all. In other words, to identify what one finds out within oneself as his reality is also the reality of all is based on the presupposition that what is there within man is also there without him. And such a presupposition not only lacks any basis or justification, but it is not Upaniṣadic. On the other hand, according to the Upaniṣads, what is there outside man is also within himself, and that is his self or *ātman* because man is an integral part of all that is there. The uniqueness of the Upaniṣadic approach lies in the Upaniṣadic quest to know *Brahman* directly and immediately. Though *Brahman* is within all yet its knowledge is direct and immediate only in relation to the reality of man.

As a matter of fact, the Upaniṣads are not intelligible and meaningful without the Vedic revelation as expressed in the Saṁhitās. In the Vedic Saṁhitās the term *brahma*, the basis for the Upaniṣadic concept of *Brahman*, is used to mean the divinely inspired devotion, and by extension to prayer, the primary means of expressing devotion, and to hymns which contain prayers. The Upaniṣads are not mystical in their approach to *Brahman*. They do not talk of any mystical experience as revealing the existence and nature of *Brahman*, nor do they describe any such experience. Nevertheless, they talk of *Brahman* that is direct and immediate, and which is present within all, including man. At the same time, the *Brahman* the Upaniṣads speak about is not a metaphysical notion or concept arrived at on the basis of man's speculative or rational understanding. The Upaniṣadic description or definition of *Brahman* as *sat*, *cit* and *ānanda* or *satyam*, *jñānam* and *anantam* is based both on direct experience and logical understanding. While *cit*, *jñānam* and *ānanda* refer to what man experiences or sees directly within himself, *satyam* and *anantam* are concepts based on man's logical understanding. And both are recognized in the Upaniṣads as essential to know *Brahman*. While the experiential basis for the Upaniṣadic concept of *Brahman* is to be found in the Vedic Saṁhitās, the logical aspect of its development is to be found in the Upaniṣadic texts. The Upaniṣads talk of *Brahman* that is direct and immediate, but have not said anything about the *Brahman*-experience which is direct and immediate. Furthermore, the Upaniṣadic realization that *Brahman* is present within man as his *ātman*, which is his real nature, is an extension of the Vedic revelation, according to which, the divine reveals itself to man by inspiring devotion (*brahma*) within him. And as nature is the direct source of divine inspiration to man he sees in nature not only its phenomenal qualities but also the presence of the divine, the real source of inspiration of devotion in man. When devotion is born in man or when he is divinely inspired he bows down in reverence to the divine, and bowing down (*namaḥ*) is the primary response of man to the divine. In almost all the Vedic hymns, *brahma* the divinely inspired devotion, its nature and meaning as well as its expression through the hymns of the Veda is talked about. But no effort is made in the Saṁhitās to understand the philosophic significance of *brahma* that is directly experienced because the Vedic Saṁhitās are primarily a collection of prayers and praises addressed to the divine or the deities. They are not speculative in their character though we find speculative hymns in the Saṁhitās which, however, end in skepticism.

The Upaniṣadic concept of *Brahman* is based directly on the Vedic *brahma*, and is developed by way of understanding the philosophic significance of Vedic *brahma*. In a sense attempts are made in the Upaniṣads to philosophically understand the truth expressed in the Vedic Saṁhitās in a poetic form and langauge. All the Vedic hymns are primarily an expression of devotion, reverence and poetic creativity. On the other hand, the Upaniṣadic verses are not hymns addressed to any deity. And some of the Upaniṣads are composed in prose form. More significantly they have no application in any Vedic ritual.

As pointed out earlier, the Upaniṣads are known primarily for their deep philosophical reflection on some of the ontological problems, as well as for their revelation of the divine and its nature within the reality of man. They form part of Vedic revelation, and reveal the nature and meaning of the divine at the human level (*adhyātma*). However, in the *Taittirīya Upaniṣad* we find certain imperative statements or commands which are definite in their meaning as they are the commands which a teacher gives to the students after the completion of studentship. Another characteristic feature of the Upaniṣads is that they have not authoritatively endorsed any view or doctrine either on the nature of reality, or on creation, or on man. Several views on any given problem are freely expressed in the Upaniṣads, and no attempt is made in them to endorse any one view or position. There is no official position or view on any ontological problem in the Upaniṣads. The fact that several, and even mutually conflicting views on several problems are presented and discussed in the Upaniṣads is a problem which has to be taken seriously in understanding the philosophy of the Upaniṣads. Can we say that all the views expressed in the Upaniṣads have the same importance and validity? Are they all equally authoritative and significant in understanding the philosophy of the Upaniṣads? If we admit that all the views expressed in the Upaniṣads are equally authoritative and valid a coherent interpretation of the Upaniṣads may not be possible because we cannot then ignore the value and significance of some views, and accept other views as true to the Upaniṣads. Keeping this problem in view some interpreters have tried to paraphrase the Upaniṣads in the name of the Philosophy of the Upaniṣads, while some have adopted an evolutionary approach to understanding the philosophy of the Upaniṣads. However, all such attempts or interpretations have something in common, and that is the presupposition that the Upaniṣads represent or stand for certain beliefs and doctrines, be it on *Brahman* or *ātman* or on creation. Attempts are, therefore, made to construct a systematic and coherent theology or philosophy of the Upaniṣads. We find several such attempts in the history of Vedānta, and almost all of them differ in their understanding of the philosophy of the Upaniṣads. Their differences are mainly due to their doctrinal or theological positions. Each interpreter could find some passage or text in support or justification of his view or interpretation or theological position. On the basis of certain Upaniṣadic passages or texts justification or validity is claimed by all the interpreters for their respective doctrinal or theological positions. The Upaniṣads thus seem to support or justify different doctrinal or theological positions even when they are in conflict with each other.

Now, it is a crucial problem whether the different interpretations of Vedānta or the different schools of Vedānta are really based on the Upaniṣads or are due to the commitment on the part of the interpreters to certain religious beliefs or theological positions which they try to justify in terms of Śruti, particularly the Upaniṣads, because of the authority they enjoy. In other words, we have to understand whether the differences in interpretation are really inspired by or based on the Upaniṣads themselves, or in the name of interpretation the Upaniṣads are adapted to justify different sectarian theological positions which may not be Upaniṣadic. This we shall discuss when we discuss the different philosophical positions which Vedānta gave rise to.

In this chapter we are mainly concerned with the philosophy of the Upaniṣads, and look to Upaniṣads for justification. In the light of the above discussion and observations we feel that the main import or intention of the Upaniṣads is not to present or propound certain doctrines or to endorse certain beliefs on any ontological or theological problem. We find several positive views on some of the ontological problems discussed in the Upaniṣads, and seldom we come across any attempt in them to reject some views in favour of other views. Different views on some of the basic ontological problems are presented and discussed without criticizing or rejecting any of them. Therefore, to assert that a certain ontological view or doctrine or a theology is true to the Upaniṣads is to impose one's view or understanding upon the Upaniṣads. But the problem whether the various views found in the Upaniṣads can be reconciled and harmonized so that a coherent philosophy of the Upaniṣads can be developed is faced by almost all the interpreters of the Upaniṣads.

If we approach the Upaniṣads without any doctrinal bias or theological commitment but keeping in view the spirit of the Vedic or Śruti tradition we feel that the Upaniṣads are not concerned with expounding certain doctrines or upholding certain beliefs or dogmas. Their chief object or purpose is to make us aware or realize for ourselves the divine or *Brahman*, the source of inspiration for the Upaniṣadic wisdom. They do not ask us to believe in or accept on their authority any doctrine or belief, or any metaphysical or theological view or position. The Upaniṣads are inspired by the divine, and the intention of the Upaniṣads is to make us realize for ourselves the divine that is present within all. The Upaniṣads express the nature of the divine, as well as the mode of its revelation at the human level. As the Upaniṣads are not prayers and praises addressed to any deity, as it is the case with the Vedic Saṁhitās, the obvious purpose of the Upaniṣads is to help us in realizing the divine for ourselves. This is the primary objective of all the Upaniṣads, and they have adopted several means to accomplish it. Much of what the Upaniṣads say is meaningful only as a means (*upāya*) or method of instruction. Therefore, the value and meaning of most of the Upaniṣadic passages are to be judged in terms of their efficacy to teach, and make us realize the divine. This seems to be the avowed purpose or objective of all the Upaniṣads, especially their famous dialogues. The Upaniṣads are meant to be taught to one who is desirous of knowing or realizing *Brahman*. This explains the place of importance given in the Upaniṣads to dialogues, examples and analogies, and graded or gradual instruction to suit the level and maturity of the taught. The purpose of Vedāntic *sādhanā*, which includes philosophical reflection, debate and discussion on several metaphysical or theological problems and doctrines, is to make one fit or competent to realize the divine that is within oneself.

The idea that though the divine is immanently present within all yet its manifestation and revelation are clear and direct in the reality of man is shared by almost all the interpreters of the Vedānta, despite their commitment to different doctrinal or theological positions. The divine immanence is central to Śruti tradition though it is expressed in different forms in different Śruti texts. We may call it the world-view or the ontological vision of the Śruti tradition. It is the basis for the unity of Śruti tradition. The divine is present within all that is there, or there is nothing in the world which is not permeated by the divine because nothing can exist without being permeated by the divine as the divine is the essence of all that is there. The divine is the inner controller as well as the unity of all that is there, and to realize for oneself the divine unity of all that is there, or the presence of the divine in all is the highest end of human existence. And the world-view is not something that can be systematized and communicated through certain definite concepts.

The Vedic hymns are poetic in form, and are in intention prayers and praises addressed to various deities either individually or collectively. We do not find in them any clear and definite statement about the divine. The variation in the language of hymns and the use of metaphors is due to differences among poet-seers of the Veda in their ability to articulate and express what is inwardly experienced. And what was expressed in a poetic form, and was meant as prayer and worship was later articulated in the Upaniṣads in a language that is mostly free from symbols and myths. The Upaniṣadic thought is more subtle, abstract and conceptual. The Upaniṣads, especially the earlier and major ones, are not *apauruṣeya* (impersonal) in the sense the Vedic hymns are. The Upaniṣadic statements about the divine and its nature are directly based on the Vedic revelation, and are in a sense re-statement of what was expressed in poetic form in the hymns of the Veda. Although based on the Vedic revelation, the Āraṇyakas and the Upaniṣads represent the Vedic wisdom as reflected upon by the seers of the Upaniṣads. They express the wisdom of the Upaniṣadic seers which is fully based on or informed by the wisdom expressed in the Vedic hymns. In a deeper sense the Upaniṣads, which belong to different Vedic Saṁhitās, present the philosophical understanding of the truth poetically expressed in the hymns of the Veda. While the Vedic hymns as prayers and praises are meant for worship of the divine, and are therefore religious, the Upaniṣads which articulate the truth revealed in and through the hymns of the Veda are not meant for religious worship. They have no ritual or religious application. They are meant to enlighten us about the divine without creating any dogmas about it. They try to help us in becoming aware of and realize for ourselves the divine and its nature, and that is regarded by the Veda as an end in itself. This is the main purpose of the Upaniṣads. They are basically texts of instruction, and are meant to teach us about the divine or *Brahman*.

The Upaniṣads are also revelatory in character, and they reveal the divine at the human level (*adhyātma*) or within the reality of man. Though the Upaniṣads are primarily concerned with the reality of man, and discovering within it the presence of the divine they contain human reflection and understanding on various ontological problems. They investigate the nature and reality of man with a view to knowing the essence (*ātman*) of man which is the divine within man. While the Vedic Saṁhitās and Brāhmaṇas are revelation of the divine at the levels of deities (*ādhidaivika*) and nature (*ādhibhautika*) the Upaniṣads are revelation of the divine at the human level (*ādhyātmika*).[8] In the Vedic Saṁhitās and Brāhmaṇas very little

8. As an integral part of the Veda the Upaniṣads form part of Vedic revelation. However, they are not revelation in the same sense as the Vedic Saṁhitās are. While in the Saṁhitās human understanding and wisdom play little or no role in the formation of the hymns, human understanding plays an important role in the Upaniṣads. Freedom of enquiry is very much encouraged in the Upaniṣads. Different and even conflicting views are freely expressed in the Upaniṣads on all important problems, and the Upaniṣads have neither favoured or accepted nor rejected any of them. Generally speaking, the Upaniṣads do not endorse any view on any problem. There are no official views in the Upaniṣads. This is mainly because the Upaniṣads are primarily concerned with teaching the nature of *Brahman* or the divine as it reveals →

is said about man and his reality. However, man is regarded in them as the best form of manifestation of the divine (*sukṛt*).[9] While each phenomenon of nature is seen as an abode of a deity, man is regarded as the abode of all the deities; in him all the deities are present. Although the divine is present within all, and reveals itself within all yet its revelation in man is more clear and perfect or complete. Man knows the world, and yet he is not satisfied with his knowledge of the world. He seeks to know what lies at the root of the world or what is not given to his sense perception or empirical experience. And the significant attributes of the divine are those that are manifest in man. The most comprehensive and abstract definition of *Brahman* attempted in the Upaniṣads, like *sat, cit* and *ānanda* (existence, consciousness and bliss) or *satyam, jñānam* and *anantam* (truth, knowledge and infinitude), represent the nature of *Brahman* as revealed within the reality of man. They are based on the revelation of the divine at the human level. While the concepts of *sat*, or *satyam* and *anantam* (existence or reality and infinitude) are based on logical understanding, and refer to what is most abstractly true of what we experience, the other concepts about *Brahman* are

→ itself at the level of human reality or within the reality of man, and for which purpose they have adopted several methods and devices. The Upaniṣads recognize the value of reason or rational understanding of man in knowing the truth. Nevertheless, they are revelation in the sense that they try to present the truth revealed in the Veda in a form which is free from myths and symbols, and is intelligible to human understanding. They are revelation as they try to reveal the nature of the divine at the human level (*ādhyātmika*) or within the reality of man. In all the famous dialogues of the Upaniṣads, and in the parable of the person from Gāndhāra we see the importance given to human understanding in knowing the truth. As a revelation of the divine at the human level or within the reality of man which is not unknown to anyone as it is the very being of man the Upaniṣads play the role of a midwife in helping one realize the truth about himself.

9. *Aitareya Āraṇyaka*, 2.3.3.3; see also *Śatapatha Brāhmaṇa* 1.4.4.7.

based on what is revealed to man within his own reality. In the world of manifestation man is the direct source of revelation of *Brahman*, and reveals the defining characteristics of *Brahman* like consciousness, bliss and knowledge. In other words, man is the best possible analogy to understand the nature of the divine as he is the best possible form of its manifestation. It is the greatness of man that he seeks to know and can also know the divine, a characteristic which is unique to man; and that is most divine in man. Knowledge is divine, and it is the unfailing light in man. Knowledge as such or in its abstract sense is the revelation of the divine. It is the divine light which illuminates and comprehends the whole world (*prajñā netram*). Man is the best form of divine manifestation, and knowledge is an essential characteristic of man. Man knows his essence, that is divine, directly and immediately as it is his being. Thus, in knowing his being man knows the divine. Otherwise, in knowing himself man comes to know himself only, or at the most what is common to all the human beings. But it is a matter of divine revelation, the essential meaning of the Veda, including the Upaniṣads, that in knowing his being man not only knows himself but also the divine, the reality of all that is there. Direct knowledge or realization of one's being is not a matter of intellectual understanding nor is it to accept on faith a theological doctrine. It is to be oneself which one is already. As man is never devoid of his being in realizing his being he does not attain anything new or what is not already attained. It is only when something new or what is not already attained is to be attained, positive instruction about what is to be attained, and how to attain it are meaningful, but not when the object of realization is one's own being. Therefore, the object of the Upaniṣadic instruction is not to make one aware of something which is otherwise unknown to him, but to awaken and guide him to his own being or reality. By means of various literary devices the Upaniṣads try to show that the divine or *Brahman* is one's own true being. Therefore, the Upaniṣadic wisdom or vision cannot be systematized and reduced to concepts or doctrines or to a theology. The Upaniṣads do not represent any metaphysics or theology. They do not teach any doctrine about *Brahman* or *ātman* or about the world. Therefore, the one who has grasped the meaning of the Upaniṣads sees or realizes the divine as his own true being as well as the inner unity of all that is there. In other words, to make one realize his true being or self is the meaning and purpose of the Upaniṣads, and they have adopted several methods or means to accomplish it. In a word, the Upaniṣads are meant to guide and make one realize that *ātman* (self) is *Brahman*. And as they do not expound any doctrine or theology the problem of systematizing their thought does not arise.

The Upaniṣadic teaching that *ātman* is *Brahman* is directly based on the Vedic revelation that *Brahman* is present within all as their essence, and is present within man as his true being or *ātman*. The Upaniṣadic revelation of *Brahman* is at the human level, and is known as *ahaṅkāra-ādeśa*[10] or *ātma-ādeśa*. The Upaniṣadic statement "you are that" is preceded by an elaborate instruction about *ātman* given to Śvetaketu by his teacher. The concluding statement of the instruction "you are that" follows the teaching about *Brahman*, namely, that "it is the essence (*ātman*) of all that is there, and that is the truth, and that is the self and "you are that" Śvetaketu."[11] Just as the tiny seed of a huge banyan tree involves the tree within itself, or is its essence so also the whole world has *Brahman* as its essence (*ātman*), and that is the truth, and that is the self (*ātman*) of Śvetaketu. Therefore, without the teaching about *Brahman*, that it is the *ātman* or essence of all, the statement "you are that" lacks justification as to why the self of man is to be regarded as the self of all which is *Brahman*. In knowing oneself (*ātman*) one knows all, and becomes all (*ahaṁ brahmasmiti sa idaṁ sarvaṁ bhavati*).[12] Self-knowledge and self-realization are given supreme importance in the Upaniṣads because one knows or realizes thereby *Brahman* which is the essence or *ātman* of all.

---

10. *Chāndogya Upaniṣad*, VII.25.1 and 2.
11. *Ibid.*, VI.1.3.
12. *BṛhUp*, 1.4.10.

"By the realization of the self through hearing, reflection and contemplation or meditation, all this is known (*idaṁ sarvaṁ viditaṁ*). All the deities, all the worlds or all that is there is known if self is known as the essence of all."[13]

Essence is that without which we cannot know a thing and its nature. If a thing cannot be known without knowing something else the latter is the essence of that thing. In the example given in illustration of the nature or meaning of essence it is said that the various particular notes played on any musical instrument have sound as their essence because they cannot be distinguished from the sound, and cannot also exist without it. The particular notes are only different forms of sound, and therefore cannot exist without sound.[14] The *Brahman* which the Upaniṣads speak about is known directly and immediately by man as his self because *Brahman* is present within all, including man. As the essence and internal ruler, *ātman* is the thread or the inner principle that unites and integrates all, and makes them one. And the one who knows that *sūtra* (thread or principle of unity) knows the worlds, knows the deities, knows the Veda, knows the beings, knows the self and knows everything.[15] The same Upaniṣad, after explaining the nature of the *sūtra* at the level of deities and the physical world, explains it at the level of man. It inhabits all the senses and faculties of man, and because of it they are able to function, and that is the *ātman*, the true being of man. This is the revelation of *Brahman* at the human level (*ādhyātmika*). It is of the nature of knowledge or consciousness (*vijñānamaya*), the light within the heart of all living beings (*prāṇeṣu hṛdyataḥ jyotiḥ puruṣa*).[16]

The dominant theme of the *Chāndogya* and *Bṛhadāraṇyaka* Upaniṣads, as far as their Upaniṣadic portions are concerned — both the Upaniṣads contain *Brahman* portions — is *Brahman*

---

13. *Ibid.*, 2.4.5, 4.3.6.
14. *Ibid.*, 2.4. pp. 7-9.
15. *Ibid.*, 3.7.1.
16. *Ibid.*, 4.3.7.

that reveals itself within the reality of man. They talk of *Brahman* as it reveals itself at the human level. This is the major or primary concern of almost all the Upaniṣads though the manner in which the problem is articulated and presented differs from Upaniṣad to Upaniṣad. In almost all the Upaniṣads the primary concern in knowing or realizing the nature of *ātman* of man is to know *Brahman* which manifests itself in man as his self or *ātman*. *Ātman*-knowledge is ontologically significant as it reveals *Brahman*. Thus, the dominant concern of all the Upaniṣads is *Brahman*, and the *Brahman* which the Upaniṣads speak about is that which is known directly and immediately as the *ātman* in man. The subtle analysis and understanding of self which we find in some of the Upaniṣads are really aimed at revealing the nature of *Brahman*.

However, the idea that the Upaniṣadic concern for the knowledge of *ātman* is for the sake of understanding the reality of man has given rise to several kinds of distortion in understanding the philosophy of the Upaniṣads. According to the Upaniṣads, the knowledge of self is not an end in itself. Upaniṣadic inquiry into the nature of self is not for the sake of understanding the reality of man, but to know and realize *Brahman* thereby. Though *Brahman* is present within all much significance is attached to the reality of man because in him the nature of *Brahman* reveals itself more clearly and fully, and man as a self-conscious being can know his essence or *ātman* directly and immediately.

Ātman-Brahman unity statements of the Upaniṣads refer to the same vision or realization as expressed by the all-*Brahman* unity statements. The intended meaning of the statement "I am *Brahman*" or "you are That" is the same as that of "all is *Brahman*." They refer to the same vision or realization though in their significance they differ. In realizing *ātman* or his true being man transcends his ordinary or empirical identity because of which he fails to recognize the inner unity or one-ness of all that is. In the *Muṇḍaka* and *Śvetāśvatara* Upaniṣads, the concern is more for understanding

Brahman who is the essence of all that is *sarvabhūtāntarātmā* (one who lives in all as their essence). *Brahman* is that which shines or reveals (*yad vibhāti*) itself in one's self as bliss and immortality. *Brahman* is known by those who know *ātman* as to know *ātman* is to know *Brahman* for all that is there is *Brahman*, and (therefore) *ātman* (of man) is *Brahman*.[17]

The purpose of this chapter is not to discuss the contents of each Upaniṣad, nor is to discuss some of the concepts like *Brahman* or *ātman* in the light of the Upaniṣads. It is also not to trace their conceptual development. The purpose is to show that the concern of the Upaniṣads in trying to know or understand the nature of *ātman* is mainly because of its capacity to reveal *Brahman* clearly and perfectly. In other words, the Upaniṣadic inquiry into the nature of *ātman* is to reveal *Brahman* at the human (*ādhyātmika*) level or within the reality of man. However, in all the attempts made by different interpreters of the Upaniṣads to build a coherent system of theology or philosophy around the concepts of *Brahman* and *ātman*, the basic concern of the Upaniṣads is lost sight of. The Upaniṣads are basically revelatory in character, and reveal *Brahman* within the reality of man or at the level of human reality. Thus, the meaning of the Upaniṣads consists in their interpretation of human existence in divine terms, or the purpose of their inquiry into the nature of human reality is to discover the divine that is within man. *Ātman* is a matter of direct realization as nowhere in the Upaniṣads *ātman* is defined or described. In a sense there can be no doctrine of *ātman* as the being of man. *Ātman* cannot be an object of knowledge or understanding. Nevertheless, in realizing one's self one comes to realize the divine or one's oneness with all that is there. This ultimately is a matter of world-view or ontological vision of the Upaniṣads which cannot be proved or justified in terms of human reason. It cannot also be defined in clear and unambiguous terms. But without grasping the world-view of the Upaniṣads there can be no understanding of the philosophy of the Upaniṣads.

---

17. *Ibid.*, 1.4.10.

3

Bādarāyaṇa

THE *Brahma-Sūtras* also known as *Vedānta-Sūtras* is the first to attempt a systematic and coherent interpretation of the Upaniṣads, as well as to provide a sort of rational justification to the Upaniṣadic thought or teaching. Although both the terms are apt to indicate the orientation and aim of the Sūtras, *Brahma-Sūtras* is more appropriate as it is primarily intended to discuss *Brahman*, its nature and meaning as well as the justification for its existence. It is basically an enquiry into *Brahman* as the *Jaiminī-Sūtras* is an enquiry into the nature of *dharma*. The primary object of the Sūtras is *Brahman*, its nature and meaning as well as the means or sources of its knowledge. All other problems such as the polemics with other schools of philosophy, cosmology, anthropology and eschatology discussed in the Sūtras gain their significance in relation to *Brahman*, and its relation to man and world. Though the Sūtras is based on the Upaniṣads the intention of the author of the Sūtras is not just to present in a systematic manner the doctrines or ideas contained in the Upaniṣads, and to provide rational justification for them, but to develop on the basis of Upaniṣads a coherent system of Vedānta philosophy.

Before we discuss the Sūtras let us first discuss a problem relevant to understanding its significance. Is it an independent inquiry into the nature and existence of *Brahman* or is it an attempt to expound the doctrine or philosophy of *Brahman*, according to the Upaniṣads? To understand the importance of the *Brahma-Sūtras* in the philosophic development of Vedānta we have to discuss whether the object of *Brahma-Sūtras* is to provide rational support and justification to the Upaniṣads, or is it an attempt to develop a coherent philosophy of the Vedānta based on both reason and the Upaniṣads? Can we say that the Sūtras is basically an attempt to interpret the Upaniṣads, or to develop a coherent system of philosophy of the Upaniṣads? This is crucial in understanding the object of the *Brahma-Sūtras* in relation to Vedānta, and its philosophic development. But how to approach this problem?

The primary object of the *Brahma-Sūtras* as stated in the beginning is to inquire into *Brahman* or the ultimate reality, the source of origin of the world, but not to understand or interpret the Upaniṣads. On the other hand, if the object of the Sūtras is to develop or expound the philosophy of the Upaniṣads, the criticism and rejection of the various views and doctrines concerning the nature of ultimate reality as developed or expounded by different schools of Indian philosophy will have no place and justification. The rival schools of philosophy are criticized and rejected on the basis of reason, but not on dogmatic grounds. The ideas and doctrines about the existence and nature of ultimate reality as represented by rival schools of philosophy are criticized and rejected in the Sūtras not because they lack scriptural support or justification, but because they lack or do not have sufficient rational justification.

We may here venture into the historical circumstances or challenges that might have influenced Bādarāyaṇa. Though much importance is given to *Brahma-Sūtras* by subsequent Vedāntins in understanding Vedānta we should not forget the fact that the *Brahma-Sūtras* does not have the status and authority of the Upaniṣads. It is not revelatory in character, but represents the wisdom of Bādarāyaṇa as well as his shortcomings. We have to understand the reasons for the emergence of the *Brahma-Sūtras*. Two reasons seem plausible, and for which we find sufficient evidence in the text of *Brahma-Sūtras*. Firstly, the broad purpose of Bādarāyaṇa, the author of *Brahma-Sūtras*, is to develop a rationally coherent philosophy of *Brahman*, which at the same time enjoys the authority of Śruti. Secondly, to enter into polemics with contending or rival systems of philosophy, especially the Sāṁkhya and Buddhist, and to criticize them and reject them so that Vedānta is firmly established. The Upaniṣads are interpreted in the *Brahma-Sūtras* in a manner that is intelligible to rational understanding of man, as well as to show or prove their significance and validity over the rival schools and doctrines. Though Sāṁkhya is not openly or explicitly based on or inspired by Śruti it has however some sort of basis or justification in Śruti. But whatever may be its basis in Śruti, Sāṁkhya is rationally meaningful and coherent, and is one of the main rivals of Vedānta. However, Kapila, its founder was esteemed and recognized as a manifestation of the divine or Viṣṇu in the Smṛti literature.[1] Now, to defend Śruti and its teaching or ideas against the rival schools of philosophy one cannot cite the authority of Śruti as the very authority of Śruti is questioned or challenged by them. It is meaningless as well as useless to cite scriptural passages against the rational arguments of the opponents, like the Sāṁkhyas and the Buddhists. If their challenge is to be met it is to be met on their own grounds. In defending Śruti or in proving its significance and validity over the rival schools of philosophy, which are based on man's rational understanding, reason is to be resorted to. It is futile to defend the Upaniṣads on dogmatic grounds or on the authority of Śruti against Sāṁkhya and Buddhism who appeal to reason for their meaningfulness and validity. Therefore, to meet the challenge of Sāṁkhya and Buddhism the Upaniṣads are to be defended on rational grounds, or their teaching or philosophy is to be shown to be rationally meaningful and valid. Bādarāyaṇa, the author of the *Brahma-Sūtras*, was well aware of the challenge to Śruti tradition in general, and the Upaniṣads in particular posed by the rival schools of philosophy, and tried to defend Śruti not dogmatically but by using the same tools and methods employed by the opponents.

1. *Bhagavad-Gītā*, Chapter 10 verse 26 (*siddhānāṁ kapilo muniḥ*).

In view of the fact that an interpretation of a tradition is influenced by the prevailing circumstances and challenges we can understand and appreciate the object or purpose of the *Brahma-Sūtras*. A tradition is interpreted from time to time keeping in view the major criticisms against it as well as to make it intelligible and meaningful in terms of the changing circumstances. An interpretation is significant when it renders the text interpreted more meaningful and intelligible in terms of the prevailing circumstances and intellectual climate. Therefore, at times, an interpretation may prove to be more meaningful than the text interpreted. The prevailing circumstances and the intellectual climate are significant and relevant in understanding and appreciating the purpose and scope of an interpretation. This also shows that no interpretation can be more authoritative than the text interpreted though in terms of intelligibility an interpretation may prove to be more significant than the text. The rules of validity that govern an interpretation cannot be applied to the text, especially when the text is religious or revealed. The authority or validity of the Śruti is not bound by time and space, and therefore no interpretation, howsoever creative it may be, can gain the status and authority of the Śruti. Even Śaṅkara's interpretation of Vedānta does not enjoy the validity of the Upaniṣads, and is not universally accepted.

Bādarāyaṇa starts his work with the *sūtra* "now let us inquire into *Brahman*" though the existence of *Brahman* and its nature is not a problem for himself as he is a follower of Śruti tradition. Why then an inquiry into *Brahman*? An inquiry into the existence and nature of a thing, or the desire to know or comprehend a thing presupposes that the inquirer though is conscious of its reality is not clearly and fully convinced about its existence and nature, or others express doubts about its reality, or there is significant and valid criticism against its reality. There can be no inquiry about a thing of which man has no knowledge whatsoever, or when a thing is known definitely and fully. This is a principle which is generally accepted by all the systems of Indian philosophy. Now,

Brahman is not a reality that is completely unknown to man. It is not a reality whose very existence is in doubt. It is a reality of which man has some kind of awareness or knowledge as all the concepts or ideas of God or the divine or *Brahman* or the ultimate reality point to the fact of its existence, though they differ in their understanding of its nature. However, in the case of *Brahma-Sūtras* inquiry into *Brahman* is more theological than metaphysical because Bādarāyaṇa depends ultimately upon the Upaniṣads to prove or establish his position rather than on reason. Therefore, his is not an autonomous or philosophic inquiry, but an inquiry based on or guided by the texts of the Upaniṣads. At the same time, it is not merely a theological exercise in the ordinary sense as its purpose is not to dogmatically uphold the Upaniṣads, and their teaching. The approach of Bādarāyaṇa in *Brahma-Sūtras* is both rational and theological, or he recognizes the importance of both reason and revelation, or *tarka* and Śruti while interpreting the Upaniṣads.

It is usually regarded that the *Brahma-Sūtras* is an attempt to present the thought of the Upaniṣads in a systematic and coherent manner as well as to reconcile the conflicting Upaniṣadic texts or ideas with a view to developing a rationally meaningful and valid philosophy of the Upaniṣads. We find in the Upaniṣads more than one view or opinion on any issue or problem, be it about *Brahman* or *ātman* or their relationship, and all the views are not compatible with each other. Several views are expressed freely in the Upaniṣads on the nature of *Brahman,* and the nature of its relationship with the world and man. We have no valid reason to doubt that they do not represent the Upaniṣadic wisdom. In view of this it would be difficult to explain why the author of the Sūtras started his inquiry with reasons or arguments for the existence of *Brahman* instead of citing textual evidence. It is difficult to decide which of the two is primary for his purpose or which of them is given more importance by him. However, the scriptural texts or statements cannot be adduced to prove *Brahman*'s existence if *Brahman* is the source of the scriptures. Then the argument will be circular. The Sūtra *śāstra yonitvāt*[2] coming as it is after certain arguments for the existence of *Brahman*, and itself forming an argument for the existence of *Brahman*, means that *Brahman* is the source of the scriptures. It can also mean that scripture is the source of *Brahman*. But following the tenor of the *Brahma-Sūtras* and its avowed object we are to accept that the intended meaning of the *sūtra* is that *Brahman* is the source of scriptures, as the *Brahma-Sūtras* starts with proving the existence of *Brahman*, and the *sūtra* is a part of that exercise. Since the intention of the *sūtra* is to provide an argument for the existence of *Brahman* it is not a simple statement, but an argument for the existence of *Brahman*. *Brahman* exists because it is the source of the scriptures.

The object of the *Brahma-Sūtras* in discussing the problem of *Brahman* is two-fold. Firstly to disprove the claim of Sāṁkhya that *pradhāna* is the ultimate reality or the ultimate source of origin of the world, as well as to show that the Sāṁkhya doctrine has no basis in the Śruti literature. Secondly, to show that all the Upaniṣadic statements in which they talk of "*prāṇa*," *vāyu, annam* as the source of the world refer to the same reality, that is, *Brahman*, though they seem to mean or refer to different things. The author of the Sūtras pays special attention to refute the view that the *pradhāna* of the Sāṁkhya is the cause of the world, and some of the Upaniṣadic statements refer to the doctrine of *pradhāna* or can be interpreted to mean the Sāṁkhya *pradhāna*. According to him, all the ontological statements of the Upaniṣads in which they talk of several things as the source of the world refer to *Brahman* which is an objectively existing reality. If the chief object of the *Brahma-Sūtras* is to present the Upaniṣadic thought in a systematic and coherent manner, as it is usually supposed, it would be difficult to understand and appreciate its concerted effort in criticizing and refuting the rival systems of philosophy, especially Sāṁkhya and Buddhist. Why should the author of the *Brahma-Sūtras* devote himself to criticizing and refuting the Sāṁkhya system of metaphysics,

2. *Brahma-Sūtras* 1.1.3 (*śāstra yonitvāt*).

as well as in proving that the Upaniṣads are not supportive of Sāṁkhya metaphysics or the Sāṁkhya metaphysics does not have any basis or support in the Upaniṣads? Further, he proved himself a best critic of rival schools of philosophy or metaphysics. His criticism and refutation of the rival schools of metaphysics was done purely on rational grounds. When he could advance cogent and strong arguments against the rival schools of philosophy or metaphysics there is no valid reason to think that he was not rational in his approach to the Upaniṣads. Instead of justifying the Upaniṣads dogmatically he tried to understand and show the limits of reason in relation to the Upaniṣadic truth.[3] However, the reasons he advances for removing the reality of *Brahman* from the purview or scope of reason are slippery. As the reality of *Brahman*, according to the Upaniṣads, is objective the rational arguments against its reality are beside the point; they will have no justification. The existence of *Brahman* is not a matter of rational proofs and arguments. It is objectively real, and is therefore a matter of direct experience. Therefore, we have to admit that the existence of *Brahman* is not a matter of rational proof or argument; it is not a metaphysical reality. This seems to have escaped the attention of Bādarāyaṇa as he starts his work with the arguments for the existence of *Brahman*. What is a matter of direct experience or what is objectively real does not depend for its existence on rational proofs or arguments. Reason cannot judge the validity of an experience, and its object. If *Brahman* is an objectively existing reality then reason has no role to play in proving or disproving its existence. In other words, the reality of *Brahman* is not a matter of man's rational understanding. *Brahman* is not a metaphysical concept, like *pradhāna*, arrived at on the basis of man's rational or speculative understanding.

Bādarāyaṇa recognizes the value of mystical experience (*ārṣa-darśna*) in validating or confirming the truth of the Upaniṣads or the reality of *Brahman*. According to him, the Upaniṣads enjoy the validity of perception in trans-empirical

---

3. *Ibid.*, 2.1.11.

matters, and reason (*anumāna*) to be significant and valid in trans-empirical matters has to base itself on the Upaniṣads. It cannot validly extend its operation beyond the realm of empirical experience, and as *Brahman* is not an empirical reality it is not within the limits of reason. Therefore, the validity of the Upaniṣads, as far as the reality of *Brahman* is concerned, does not depend on rational justification or support; the authority of the Upaniṣads is supreme and final as far as the reality of *Brahman* is concerned. However, this cannot be the case with Sāṁkhya as it is based on man's rational understanding, and therefore the validity of its concepts can be accepted or rejected on rational grounds. Thus, the approach of Bādarāyaṇa to the problem of *Brahman*'s existence is highly significant and well-founded.

Bādarāyaṇa is also known for his attempts at reconciling the various Upaniṣadic texts and statements. In the history of Vedānta, a significant attempt is made in the *Brahma-Sūtras* to reconcile the various Upaniṣadic statements or views which are not compatible with each other, and thus to develop a coherent philosophy of the Upaniṣads. Being fully aware of the philosophical or logical problems the Upaniṣads give rise to Bādarāyaṇa was the first to deal with them systematically, and to discuss them in a rationally intelligible manner. His approach to the problem of reconciliation is rational, and that is his significant contribution to the philosophical development of Vedānta. The problem that has attracted the attention of all the Vedāntins, and proved itself crucial in the philosophical development of Vedānta is the problem of reconciliation of the mutually conflicting Upaniṣadic statements and views. Problems of philosophic significance arise in any attempt to reconcile and harmonize the mutually conflicting Upaniṣadic texts and statements, and more so when the attempt is in terms of reason. The rational approach of Bādarāyaṇa to the problem of reconciliation has given rise to certain philosophical problems with which we are now concerned.

At the outset we have to admit that all the Upaniṣadic statements cannot have the same authority and validity as they not only agree among themselves but even contradict each other. And without their reconciliation it is not possible to systematize the Upaniṣadic thought, and develop a coherent philosophy of the Upaniṣads. In such a situation Bādarāyaṇa seems to have realized the significance of reason in achieving reconciliation between the Upaniṣadic statements that conflict with each other. He employed reason freely while criticizing the rival systems of philosophy, which is justified as in certain cases, like Sāṁkhya, the ideas and doctrines are based on speculative reasoning. But how we can justify a purely rational approach to understand Buddhism and its truth? If we admit that the philosophical positions of different schools of Buddhism are either directly or indirectly based on or are inspired by the truth realized by the Buddha in the state of enlightenment, their validity does not depend on reason alone. The ontological position of the Buddhists is based more on the personal realization or enlightenment of the Buddha than on the argumentative skills of different Buddhist philosophers. Therefore, the ontological position of Buddhism is in a real sense a rival to that of the Upaniṣads as both of them are not based entirely on speculative reasoning. Keeping this in view the author of the *Brahma-Sūtras* should have shown the same reverence and adopted the same approach towards Buddhism and its philosophy as he did towards Upaniṣads and their teaching. Instead, he has adopted the same approach which he has adopted towards Sāṁkhya in understanding and criticizing Buddhism. Had Bādarāyaṇa adopted the same approach to the Upaniṣads and Buddhism and avoided a purely rational understanding and criticism of Buddhist philosophy, as it is also based on the personal realization of the Buddha, then his analysis and understanding of reason and its limits would have been really objective. Instead he sees the limitations of reason only in relation to the Upaniṣadic truth, but not in relation to other similar claims and positions like those of Buddhism and Jainism. The Buddhist analysis and criticism of all metaphysical claims and positions is not based completely on reason, but directly or indirectly on the enlightening experience of the Buddha which as a direct experience is as valid and significant as that of Vāmadeva and other Upaniṣadic seers.[4] On the other hand, unbridled use of reason is fully justified in criticizing and rejecting the metaphysical claims and positions which are based on reason alone. As far as Sāṁkhya is concerned it is a system of philosophy based on reason as arguments are developed to prove its basic claims though the Smṛti tradition recognizes Kapila, the founder of Sāṁkhya, as a seer or a sage. In all the arguments developed by Sāṁkhya to prove the existence of either *puruṣa* or *prakṛti* it has not referred to any non-rational source or to any mystical or revealed experience. However, it is a fact that the Sāṁkhya concept of *prakṛti* and the arguments for its existence are adopted by almost all the schools of Indian philosophy.

The more significant attempt on the part of Bādarāyaṇa is to defend the Vedāntic ontology against that of Sāṁkhya which he has done by way of interpreting the Upaniṣads. In this connection we have to understand whether the Upaniṣads represent or uphold any philosophical position or doctrine either about *Brahman* or *ātman* or about their relationship. Can we justifiably develop a system of metaphysics on the basis of the Upaniṣads? Is it possible to build a systematic and coherent system of philosophy on the basis of the Upaniṣads? One's attitude to these problems depends upon one's approach to

4. All the schools of Buddhist philosophy are developed on the basis of or inspired by the Buddha's experience of *nirvāṇa*. They are the different ways of understanding the philosophical significance of *nirvāṇa*, or they try to find out the philosophical implications of *nirvāṇa* to various problems of philosophy. They are not developed purely on the basis of speculative reason, and cannot therefore be viewed and criticized as having no other significance to human life than that of logical coherence and validity. They are the different ways of understanding the significance of *nirvāṇa* to various problems of philosophy. Though they follow the method of logical analysis they are in the final analysis an attempt to find out the implications of *nirvāṇa* to various problems of philosophy.

and understanding of the Upaniṣads. Are the Upaniṣads a source of knowledge of *Brahman* or *ātman* and their relationship which can be conceptualized and communicated? One's interpretation of the Upaniṣads depends upon one's attitude towards them. It is somewhat like the modern debate whether the Veda stands for polytheism or monotheism in which people are influenced or guided by their own world-views. If someone thinks that the Upaniṣads are a source of knowledge of *Brahman* or *ātman* or of their relationship which leads to liberation then one may interpret the Upaniṣads with a view to presenting that knowledge in a clear and definite manner. On the other hand, if one's understanding of the Upaniṣads is that they have no specific doctrines or views to uphold, either on *Brahman* or on *ātman* or on their relationship, but are intended to help us in realizing for ourselves the divine or *Brahman* that is present within us his approach to the Upaniṣads will be radically different.

Almost all the schools of Vedānta accept that the Upaniṣads are a source of valid knowledge of *Brahman*, and therefore they try to show that all the ontological statements of the Upaniṣads really refer to *Brahman*, and this they try to prove by interpreting the Upaniṣads. For instance, in some Upaniṣads, *Brahman* or ultimate reality is defined in terms of *prāṇa* or *vāyu*, or is identified as Prajāpati, Hiraṇyagarbha, etc. in some other Upaniṣads it is defined in terms of *Sat*, *cit*, *ānanda* or truth, knowledge and infinitude. While in some Upaniṣads the cause of the universe is identified as Prajāpati or Hiraṇyagarbha or Īśvara, in some others an indeterminate or indefinable reality known as *Brahman* is seen as the source of the world. But in some other Upaniṣads any kind of causal relationship between *Brahman* and the world is denied. The world is not seen as a created or caused reality, but as a spontaneous self-manifestation or expression of *Brahman*, like the growth of hair on a living human body or as spider weaving a web.[5] Now as long as the terms or concepts like Īśvara,

---

5. *Muṇḍaka Upaniṣad* 1.1.7; see also *Bṛhadāraṇyaka* Upaniṣad 2.1.20.

Prajāpati, etc. carry their meanings they cannot be construed as referring to the same reality. And even if we can somehow show that they all refer to the same reality, the reality so referred to cannot have a definite meaning or definition. It can mean several things to several persons. If reality can mean different things to different people it may not have objective reality.

As pointed out later by Śaṅkara some of the Upaniṣadic statements, though few in number, deny validity to most of the Upaniṣadic statements, and therefore both cannot be accorded the same kind of validity and authority. They also cannot be reconciled in terms of reason. Similar is the case with the Upaniṣadic statements that deal with *Brahman* or *ātman* or the world of empirical experience and the way they are related. For instance, the Upaniṣads present several views about the relationship between *Brahman* and the world, and in certain statements in which the existence of the world is likened to the breathing process of *Brahman* deny any kind of causal relationship between them. The world of empirical experience is not seen as different from *Brahman* as it is seen as a spontaneous self-manifestation of *Brahman*. About *ātman* one thing is clearly and definitely stated in the Upaniṣads. *Ātman* is used to mean the essence of a thing or a phenomenon, and is therefore present within all. And in man it is known as his self. While in man *ātman* reveals itself as his self, in other phenomena it reveals itself in different ways. In other words, *ātman* is present not only within man, but in all or in everything as essence. And as *Brahman* is known or reveals itself within the world of empirical experience as *ātman* it is present within all. It is not only the self of man that is one with *Brahman* but the whole world is one with *Brahman* as *Brahman* is the essential oneness of all. When such an obvious view of the Upaniṣads is overlooked in understanding the meaning and nature of *ātman* certain problems arise in under-standing the Upaniṣads, and they cannot be overcome or surmounted by way of interpreting the Upaniṣadic texts in a technical sense. All the Upaniṣadic statements on *ātman* cannot have the same meaning. In some statements it is used to mean essence in which sense *ātman* is present within all as their essence. And as the essence of man *ātman* is his self. As *Brahman* is present within all as essence (*ātman*), *ātman* is *Brahman* in a very natural sense. In this sense *ātman* is used to mean the essence or reality of all. *Ātman* is also used to mean what one thinks of oneself. We find the same problem with regard to *Brahman*. All the Upaniṣadic statements about *Brahman* cannot have the same meaning, or cannot in their plain meaning refer to the same reality. The Upaniṣadic terms for the ultimate reality or the ultimate source of the world like, *Brahman*, *ātman*, Prajāpati, Īśvara, etc. are concepts having their own meanings, and cannot therefore mean one and the same thing.

However, we can understand and appreciate Bādarāyaṇa in his efforts to develop a systematic and coherent philosophy of the Upaniṣads with a view to defending the Upaniṣads against the rival systems of philosophy, like Sāṁkhya and Buddhism. In defending the Vedānta he wanted to defend the Śruti tradition against Sāṁkhya and Buddhism. The Sāṁkhya philosophy and the different schools of Buddhist philosophy which Bādarāyaṇa discusses are coherent systems of metaphysical thought well argued and justified. They are rationally intelligible, and are rationally justifiable. Therefore, to defend the Śruti tradition, particularly the Upaniṣads, against Sāṁkhya and Buddhism it is not sufficient to criticize them, and deny validity to them dogmatically or on the authority of the Śruti texts. One has to offer an alternative system of metaphysics which is free from the fallacies of systems criticized and rejected. It cannot be another system of philosophy or metaphysics based purely on reason as no such system of metaphysics can be objective and universal in its meaning and validity. Therefore, the aim of *Brahma-Sūtras* is to develop a system of philosophy based on both reason and Śruti, or to develop a philosophy of the Upaniṣads which is rationally coherent and valid. Most of the Upaniṣadic texts and statements do not agree among themselves or are not consistent with each other on some of the basic problems.

They not only disagree among themselves on certain basic problems but even contradict each other. Furthermore, it is not easy to determine what the Upaniṣads represent or what the Upaniṣadic statements really state about *Brahman* or *ātman* or about their relationship. Another problem with the Upaniṣads is that they are not definite and consistent in their views about anything. And most of the Upaniṣadic statements are ambiguous in the sense that it is difficult to find out whether they are literally true or are only true metaphorically. They do not contain definite propositions about anything, so that the truth they represent can be logically related and presented in a coherent way. For instance, in the Sāṁkhya system of philosophy from the definition given of *prakṛti* or *puruṣa* certain things can be deducted logically. But it is not the case with the concept of *Brahman* or *ātman* of the Upaniṣads, so that a systematic and logically coherent system of metaphysics can be built around them. In this context it may not be out of place to say something about *Brahman*. In the Vedic-Saṁhitās *brahma*, the basis or the source of origin or inspiration for the Upaniṣadic *Brahman*, primarily means divinely inspired devotion as well as its expression in prayer or Vedic hymn. A prayer which finds its expression through a Vedic hymn is due to devotion which is divinely inspired. But what devotion is cannot be defined in clear terms, and conceptualized. It is not a metaphysical principle, nor a category of explanation of anything. It refers to what is inwardly experienced, and according to the seers of the Veda, it is due to divine inspiration. Devotion is divine, and in the state of devotion everything is seen as divine, or man's attitude towards the world is transformed and acquires a new or divine meaning or significance. Therefore, *brahma* in the Veda is not a metaphysical principle or notion conceived to explain anything. With the birth of devotion human life is supremely fulfilled, or man realizes the ultimate meaning of his life. The Vedic hymns as prayers addressed to different deities, either individually or collectively, express *brahma*. And the Vedic-Saṁhitās are a collection of hymns or prayers, and are meant for the worship of the divine.

The Upaniṣads differ from the Saṁhitās in an important sense though both form part of the Veda, and represent the same wisdom or world-view which is reflected in all the Vedic literature. The Upaniṣads are partly an attempt to understand the philosophical significance of the Vedic *brahma*, and partly a revelation of *Brahman* at the human level. In the process of understanding the philosophic significance of *brahma* they have tried to conceptualize it and define it. Nevertheless, the Upaniṣads are not oblivious to the fact that *Brahman* is basically a matter of direct and immediate experience or realization though such an experience is not described in the texts of the Upaniṣads. Thus, the *Brahman* of the Upaniṣads is formed and developed on the basis of Vedic *brahma* which is an inspired experience. Though the *Brahman* of the Upaniṣads is based on Vedic revelation, in its formation rational understanding of man has played its role. We have to keep this in mind to understand and appreciate the Upaniṣadic view that though the concept of *Brahman* is intelligible to rational understanding of man yet conceptual understanding alone is not sufficient or adequate to know *Brahman*. *Brahman* is beyond or transcends all the concepts developed to determine and define its nature. They can only point to or indicate *Brahman* without making it their object. The Upaniṣadic concept of *Brahman* which is based directly on *brahma* is a matter of direct experience, and is therefore not a metaphysical concept developed to explain anything.

However, the Vedic *brahma* has a philosophical significance, and that is its immanent character. The immediate source of its inspiration to man is nature in all its phenomena. The source of its inspiration is not limited to any one phenomenon of nature. As the divine that is present in nature is the source of inspiration of *brahma* the divine is seen as dwelling within nature. The Vedic *brahma* which is a matter of direct experience may, however, give rise to certain philosophical problems such as its relation to nature, its significance in understanding nature and its ontological status and validity. These are matters of man's rational understanding, as well as the basis for the emergence of various concepts of the divine or *Brahman*. If we can understand the emergence of concepts and doctrines based on *brahma* we can understand the relationship between the two. The concepts or doctrines about *Brahman* though based on Vedic *brahma* cannot be regarded as logically related to it. There can be no logical relationship between *brahma* and the various concepts or doctrines it is supposed to have given birth to; they cannot be logically developed on the basis of *brahma*. Even the Upaniṣadic statement "all is *Brahman*" is made by way of understanding the significance of *brahma*. Therefore, the need must have been felt by some of the philosophers of Vedānta to interpret the Upaniṣadic statements about *Brahman*, to clear or remove the fallacies which a rational understanding of *Brahman* gives rise to.

The divinely inspired devotion which the Vedic hymns describe is not an experience in the ordinary sense. The presence of the divine in nature is experienced in the state of devotion which transforms one's vision and understanding, and *Brahman* stands for such a vision or world-view. *Brahman* is not, therefore, a metaphysical concept around which a system of philosophy can be built. It may however inspire a doctrine or a theology. But the concepts or doctrines or theologies supposedly based on the vision or world-view cannot be logically related to it, or cannot strictly speaking be derived from it. It can influence man's understanding about the world and its meaning. And depending upon one's understanding and appreciation of the vision or world-view it is interpreted. It can, therefore, give rise to several interpretations without itself being logically tied to any one interpretation.

The Upaniṣads can only point to *Brahman* or inspire one to the vision or world-view commonly expressed in all the Upaniṣads. They are not intended to communicate any dogmas or doctrines about *Brahman* or *ātman*. They have only instructional or means value. The Upaniṣads are meant to teach or instruct, and for that purpose they adopt various means and ways. Therefore, the Upaniṣadic statements are not to be taken as literally true, and interpreted. When the world-view of the Upaniṣads is realized they serve their purpose and cease to be valid which is meaningful only when the Upaniṣadic statements are not literally true. They are valid to the extent they are capable of inspiring one to their world-view or vision. All the Upaniṣadic statements ultimately refer or point to the same truth that is *Brahman*, as according to the Upaniṣadic world-view, all that is there is permeated by *Brahman* or is *Brahman*. Otherwise, we cannot say that all the Upaniṣadic statements refer to the same reality or *Brahman*. All that is there is *Brahman* or *Brahman* is all that is there is a vision or a world-view that is commonly reflected in the entire Śruti tradition, though it is articulated and expressed more clearly and conceptually in the Upaniṣads. Independently of the world-view most of the Upaniṣadic statements will not be meaningful and valid. Though the Upaniṣads aim at inspiring or imparting the vision or world-view some of their statements are more significant in expressing it. Therefore, reconciliation of the Upaniṣadic statements is possible only in the light of the world-view, as the ultimate purpose of all the Upaniṣads is to express the world-view but not to advocate this or that doctrine. The immanent nature of the divine or its being the inner unity of all that is there is the vision or world-view of the Upaniṣads, and therefore without appreciating the world-view of the Upaniṣads we cannot understand their meaning or philosophy. The oneness of the divine which reveals itself in and through all the realms of the universe is the meaning or wisdom of Śruti or its world-view. The Upaniṣads reveal the divine at the human level while the other Śruti texts reveal the divine at the other two levels. The world-view of the Upaniṣads confers validity and meaning to all the Upaniṣadic statements, and as all the statements of the Upaniṣads aim at expressing the world-view there is no problem of conflict among them. The problem of conflict arises only when we try to understand the meaning of Upaniṣadic statements individually and independently of the Upaniṣadic vision or world-view. Therefore, the problem of reconciliation of the conflicting

Upaniṣadic statements can be avoided by pointing to the world-view of the Upaniṣads which all the texts and statements in unison convey. On the other hand, conflict is possible only when the Upaniṣadic statements are taken to be literally true, and are seen as communicating certain doctrines.

If the Upaniṣads do not represent any theology or a set of doctrines but a vision or world-view the purpose of interpretation will be different. On the other hand, if the Upaniṣads are seen as communicating the knowledge of *Brahman* or *ātman* or their relationship in the ordinary sense of knowledge then the object of interpretation will be different. Then the purpose of interpretation will be to develop a coherent system of metaphysics or theology on the basis of the Upaniṣads. In that case the problem of reconciliation of various Upaniṣadic statements that are not compatible with each other will be a formidable one. And the metaphysics so developed will not be significantly different from other systems of metaphysics. If the object of the Upaniṣads is not to communicate certain doctrines but to awaken man or inspire him to a world-view or vision the problem of interpretation will be to free a person from the snare and attachment to certain dogmas or doctrines, and help him to see the truth of the Upaniṣads for himself. A world-view or an ontological vision is not amenable to systematization and conceptualization. Therefore, any attempt to build a systematic and coherent metaphysics on the basis of Upaniṣads will miss the basic purpose of the Upaniṣads, and end up in distorting their meaning. Even when we try to conceptualize the world-view of the Upaniṣads or construct a system of metaphysics around the Upaniṣads sufficient care should be taken to make such a system open ended, or without giving rise to any rigid or dogmatic beliefs and doctrines.

4

Śaṅkara

Before we discuss the place of importance of Śaṅkara in the philosophical development of Vedānta we have to keep in mind that he alone among the interpreters of Vedānta commented upon all the three basic sources of Vedānta, namely, the Upaniṣads, *Brahma-Sūtras* and the *Bhagavad-Gītā*. And his commentaries on all the three are extensive. Among the three fundamental sources of the Vedānta, known as *Prasthānatrayī* it is the Upaniṣads that belong to Śruti tradition, while the *Bhagavad-Gītā* and the *Brahma-Sūtras* belong to Smṛti tradition. The latter two acknowledge that they are based on or are inspired by the Śruti, especially the Upaniṣads. While the *Brahma-Sūtras* is obviously an attempt to present systematically and coherently the thought or philosophy of the Upaniṣads, the *Bhagavad-Gītā* regards itself as the essence of the Upaniṣads, and even regards itself as an Upaniṣad. Apart from the historical reasons for the emergence of the *Bhagavad-Gītā* and *Brahma-Sūtras*, both of them in their own characteristic ways try to represent the world-view of the Upaniṣads. In that respect, they do not differ or deviate from the Upaniṣads. However, they show or maintain their individuality when they discuss and interpret certain problems of Vedānta, as well as in the ways in which they try to reconcile the views or ideas of the Śruti tradition which are not compatible with each other. Each is a great text, and has an identity of its own. While the *Brahma-Sūtras* depends upon the Upaniṣads for its meaning and validity, *Bhagavad-Gītā* is a text which to a large extent is meaningful by itself. Its approach to and understanding of the problems it discusses are its own. Nevertheless, they both share something in common. While the *Brahma-Sūtras* marks the beginning of the process of reconciliation of mutually conflicting views and texts of Śruti, particularly the Upaniṣads, the process of reconciliation is carried forward by the author of the *Bhagavad-Gītā*, and more significantly the process of reconciliation is extended to cover or include the Smṛti tradition. The *Bhagavad-Gītā* is an attempt, *par excellence*, to reconcile the traditions of Śruti and Smṛti without undermining the importance of either. The genius of Vyāsa, a master reconciler of different traditions and views, is fully reflected in the text of *Bhagavad-Gītā*. The process of reconciliation initiated by Vyāsa has become the ideal for several Vedāntins who in their own ways tried to reconcile not only the Upaniṣadic texts and statements which are not compatible with each other, but different sectarian traditions of Smṛti tradition, like Śaivism, Vaiṣṇavism and Śāktism with Vedānta. Such attempts though are worthy of recognition and appreciation from a religious or theological point of view fail to have universal appeal and philosophical justification for which the Upaniṣads are known. In their zeal or enthusiasm to adapt the Upaniṣads to meet certain sectarian theological demands, or to reconcile sectarian theologies with the ontology of the Upaniṣads they compromise with the universal or non-sectarian character and appeal of the Upaniṣads. In a sense, the non-sectarian Upaniṣads are made to lend their authority and support to sectarian theological claims of Smṛti tradition.

In the history of Vedānta the *Brahma-Sūtras*, though strictly speaking a secondary source, has become for many Vedāntins a primary source. All the Vedāntins down to Radhakrishnan commented upon the *Brahma-Sūtras*. However, it is only Śaṅkara who has commented upon all the important and major Upaniṣads besides an extensive and comprehensive commentary on the other two sources of Vedānta, namely *Bhagavad-Gītā* and *Brahma-Sūtras*. It is not easy to determine why most of the Vedāntins preferred to comment on the *Brahma-Sūtras* rather than on the Upaniṣads. However, because of the cryptic nature of the Sūtras, and the ambiguity involved in their meaning, the *Brahma-Sūtras* is amenable to different interpretations. As *Brahma-Sūtras* is also polemical its different interpreters find it easy to indulge in polemics against rival interpretations of Vedānta, especially that of Śaṅkara. While Bādarāyaṇa entered into polemics against rival schools of philosophy, like Sāṁkhya and Buddhism, most of the important post-Śaṅkara interpreters of *Brahma-Sūtras* directed their criticism against the interpretation of Śaṅkara. All this is possible mainly because the *Brahma-Sūtras* is amenable to such interpretations.

It is only Śaṅkara who has tried to interpret or has made an attempt to understand the meaning of the Upaniṣads directly instead of depending upon the interpretation of others. He commented upon both the Upaniṣads and the *Brahma-Sūtras*. Is it then redundant on his part to comment on the *Brahma-Sūtras*? Can one understand the philosophy of the Upaniṣads independently or without the help of the *Brahma-Sūtras*? Can we say that the *Brahma-Sūtras* is the most significant and authoritative interpretation of the Upaniṣads? Is *Brahma-Sūtras* adequate or sufficient to understand the philosophy of the Upaniṣads? But no Vedāntin will admit that the *Brahma-Sūtras* is as authoritative as the Upaniṣads in understanding Vedānta, because the *Brahma-Sūtras* itself admits its dependence on the Upaniṣads. An important problem that naturally arises in this context is whether the Upaniṣads are aware of their own shortcomings or inner contradictions. The Upaniṣads do not represent the wisdom of any one person or seer. They express different views on any problem or issue, and are not afraid of making contradictory statements on any problem. Apparently they do not have inner cohesion, nor do they seem to represent any one belief or doctrine about *Brahman* or *ātman* or their relationship. Can we, therefore, say that the Upaniṣads have no unity of thought or vision? Is there anything that is common to all the Upaniṣads, and make them belong to one genre of literature? Are they conscious of the unity of their vision? Can we say, on the other hand, that the conflict among the ideas and statements we find in the Upaniṣads does not really vitiate the unity or vision of the Upaniṣads? Do we find in the Upaniṣads any method of reconciliation of the mutually conflicting views or statements?

One way of understanding the problem of conflict or contradiction among the statements of the Upaniṣads is to point out the fact that the Upaniṣads do not represent the wisdom of anyone person or seer. The Upaniṣads reflect the wisdom of several persons or seers, and therefore the contradictions are not really significant. They are to be taken seriously only when the wisdom expressed in the Upaniṣads emanates from one and the same person. The wisdom of one person may not be completely consistent or compatible with that of other persons. And as the Upaniṣads represent the wisdom of several persons or seers belonging to different periods of time contradictions found in them need not be taken seriously. On the other hand, contradiction will be a serious problem when the same person expresses several views on any problem which are not compatible with each other. For instance, Sāṁkhya is not a contradiction of Vedānta, nor Vedānta a contradiction of some other philosophy. They represent different points of view or different approaches to understand the problem which in a sense is identical. Therefore, they can co-exist without undermining the significance and validity of each other. This type of approach could be a possible solution to the problem of reconciliation. For instance, there are several views expressed in the Upaniṣads about the origin of the world which are not compatible with each other. Similarly, there are several views about the nature of *Brahman*. However, as the views are about the same thing or problem, and as they do not agree with each other the problem of conflict arises. If one is taken to be true the others cannot be true. Therefore, all the views expressed in the Upaniṣads either about the origin of the world or about the nature of *Brahman* cannot be true. And if we want to find out the truth of the Upaniṣads we have to, as a first step, reconcile the various statements that are in conflict with each other.

Some interpreters of the Vedānta have adopted the method of evolution or development to overcome the problem of contradiction. All the views expressed in the Upaniṣads, on any problem, need not have the same authority and validity. There are views which are primitive or undeveloped, and are therefore historical in their value and significance. They do not therefore contradict those views which are well developed. On the other hand, if by development we mean the logical development we have to compromise with the Śruti or revelatory character of the Upaniṣads. Moreover, it would be difficult to foresee and determine the final outcome of the process of logical development of any idea. Now, can we say that the Śruti character of the Upaniṣads is compatible with the process of logical development of its ideas and doctrines? This seems to be the crux of the problem. How far can we extend reason in comprehending the meaning of the Upaniṣads, as well as their coherence and validity? In other words, what could be the role of reason in developing a systematic and coherent philosophy of the Upaniṣads? Can we say that all the Upaniṣadic statements do not have the same authority and validity? If some of the Upaniṣadic statements do not have the same validity and authority as some other statements have, how to explain the significance and role of such statements in the Upaniṣads?

Another major problem we have to consider in this connection is whether the Upaniṣadic statements or insights can be used to develop a logically coherent system of philosophy, or more specifically a system of metaphysics. For instance, how to determine the nature and status of the Upaniṣadic statements like "all is *Brahman*?" Are they metaphysical in character, or are they based on speculative reasoning? Can we say that the status of *Brahman* is like that of Sāṁkhya *prakṛti* or *puruṣa* from which certain things can be logically deducted? Sāṁkhya has developed various arguments to prove the existence of *prakṛti* and *puruṣa*, but nowhere in the Upaniṣads we find any attempt to prove or provide rational justification for the statements like, "all is *Brahman*." At the same time, they are not statements expressing revealed truths because the Veda is not revelation in the ordinary or Semitic sense. They are also not statements describing any mystical experience. No mystical experience can have "all" as its object as "all" is a synonym of *Brahman*, one without a second. In the statement "all is *Brahman,*" "all" is used to include all that is there. Furthermore, according to the Veda, the divine or *Brahman* is self-revealing by its very nature. It is ever revealing, and reveals itself to those who can see. The Vedic revelation involves such "seeing." As an integral part of the Veda the Upaniṣads continue the same tradition. Therefore, the Upaniṣadic statements like "all is *Brahman*" express such "seeing," or the vision or the world-view of the Upaniṣads. We do not find any arguments in the Upaniṣads in support or justification of the vision or world-view. The Upaniṣadic statements, especially those that are regarded as cardinal, express the ontological vision or the world-view of the Upaniṣads. And as the vision or world-view is not created or shaped by human reason it does not depend for its justification on human reason.

We do not also have any evidence in the Upaniṣads to show that the thought they contain is metaphysical, or is based on rational understanding of man. We cannot, therefore, say that its coherence is logical. We do not also come across in the Upaniṣads any attempt to reconcile and harmonize the views expressed in them. However, all the statements of the Upaniṣads do not have the same status and authority. This is mainly because the main purpose of the Upaniṣads is to teach the nature of *Brahman* that is present within one's being, but not to prove its existence as if it is an object of human knowledge or understanding. The object of almost all the Upaniṣads, particularly the major Upaniṣads like *Chāndogya* and *Bṛhadāraṇyaka*, is to show the nature of *Brahman* that is present within man with the help of appropriate examples and analogies. Therefore, the language used, and the different examples and analogies employed to teach the nature of *Brahman* should not be taken in their literal sense. They are not literally true as their purpose or intention is not to describe but to show and teach. And their purpose is served when one realizes the truth about himself or *ātman* directly. Most of the Upaniṣadic passages and dialogues, analogies and examples which are invented or devised to teach or instruct the nature of *Brahman* cannot, therefore, be used either to justify or criticize a metaphysical view or position.

We come across in the Upaniṣads another kind of statements which indicate the choice of a person regarding the object of his worship or meditation (*upāsanā*). In several of the Upaniṣadic passages different persons indicate their choice about the nature or identity of *Brahman* or the deity with which it is identified mainly for the purpose of worship or meditation. Some may meditate on mind as *Brahman*, or on the sun as *Brahman*, or on *vāyu* as *Brahman*, etc. just as *vāk* (speech) is meditated upon as *dhenu* (cow), or an idol is worshipped as a deity (*mano brahmeti upāsita ādityaṁ brahmeti upāsita*).[1] In all such statements in which *Brahman* is worshipped or meditated upon as mind, or the sun, or *prāṇa*, etc. the intention is not to describe or define the nature of *Brahman*. They serve a practical religious purpose, and have therefore practical significance or meaning as different people choose different deities and identify them as *Brahman* for the practical purpose of worship or meditation. Such statements cannot be taken to define or describe *Brahman*, or as an authority to reveal the nature of *Brahman*. Such statements as well as the statements of instruction are not literally meaningful and true. They are pedagogic in nature, and serve the practical purpose of instruction or meditation or worship. In other words, the above kind of statements which abound in the Upaniṣads cannot have the same status, authority and validity as some other statements in which the nature of *Brahman* is sought to be indicated or defined. They are not revelatory in character, and cannot therefore have authority either to justify or criticize any ontological position. In this connection we can refer to

1. *Chāndogya Upaniṣad* 3.8.1, 3.19.4; *Bṛhadāraṇyaka Upaniṣad* 5.8.1.

those Brāhmaṇa texts, which the *Chāndogya* and *Bṛhadarāṇyaka* Upaniṣads contain, and have only liturgical value.

The passages of the *Bṛhadarāṇyaka* and *Kena* Upaniṣads in which *ātman* is defined as the subject of knowledge and experience, but not as an object of knowledge or experience are intended to show or teach the nature of *ātman*, the reality of man which is ever revealed. The *Brahman*, that is present within all as their essence is present within man, and is known as his self or *ātman*. The Upaniṣadic statements like "all is *Brahman*," "I am *Brahman*," etc. which are a few in number express clearly the world-view or the ontological vision of the Upaniṣads, and are therefore regarded as cardinal or central to understanding the meaning of the Upaniṣads. And almost all the Vedāntins differ in their interpretation of those cardinal statements, and depending upon the differences in interpretation different schools of Vedānta are born. Though the Upaniṣads are regarded as revelation of *Brahman* at the human level (*ādhyātmika*) in significance the revelation of *Brahman* is the same as that of revelation of *Brahman* at the other two levels of *ādhidaivika* and *ādhibhautika*. They all reflect and express the same vision or world-view.

The purport of the major Upaniṣadic statements like "I am *Brahman*," "all is *Brahman*," "you are That," is the same as they all express the same vision or world-view. To see or realize the divine within oneself is the same as to realize or see its presence within all, or to realize the divine within all is the same as to realize its presence within oneself. They are two ways of understanding the same vision. All that is there is permeated by the divine is central to the world-view of Śruti tradition, including the Upaniṣads, and that is expressed succinctly by all the cardinal statements of the Upaniṣads.

When Śaṅkara makes a distinction between the Upaniṣadic statements in which the divine or *Brahman* is spoken as an object of worship or meditation (*upāsanā*), and the statements in which *Brahman* is spoken as an object of direct realization, he refers to two kinds of Upaniṣadic statements which do not have the same status, authority and validity. They should not be mixed up or confused in understanding the Upaniṣads as both do not have the same kind of authority and validity. The *upāsanā* statements of the Upaniṣads do not have objective validity as the object of meditation or worship depends upon an individual's choice. But what is commonly reflected in all the texts of the Upaniṣads, and unifies them is the vision or the world-view that the divine or *Brahman* is immanently present within all. When *Brahman* is present within all it can be meditated upon in the form of any deity provided such meditation does not lead to sectarian views about the nature of *Brahman*, or identification of *Brahman* with the deity of worship.

Similarly, the statements of instruction or the statements meant for teaching which also abound in the Upaniṣads do not have ontological validity. They are not intended to support or justify or oppose or criticize any ontological view or position. They are of instructional or means value, and cease to be significant and valid the moment truth is grasped and realized. Furthermore, the method of instruction can change from teacher to teacher, and also depends upon the level of the student. In a broader sense the Upaniṣads are really meant for teaching. They are of instructional or pedagogic value, as in reality the truth which the Upaniṣads teach is ever revealed. Therefore, most of the Upaniṣadic statements can have only means (*upāya*) or instructional value, and practical validity. The instruction is effective when it succeeds in making the student comprehend the meaning of what is taught or instructed. As the purpose of instruction is to make one grasp the object of instruction, the significance of instruction lies in its efficacy to communicate and make one grasp or comprehend the meaning of what is taught. For instance, in teaching alphabets different languages invent different signs for letters, and the signs will have only practical value and significance. They can be changed or altered. The method of instruction depends upon the ingenuity of the teacher and the level of the student, and can therefore be adjusted according to the need and situation. And most of the Upaniṣadic statements and dialogues are not intended to expound or justify any philosophical or theological view of position. They cannot therefore be used to justify or criticize any doctrine or view.

As pointed out earlier, the cardinal statements of the Upaniṣads, which are a few in number, express the vision or world-view of the Upaniṣads succinctly. Their validity does not depend upon any given situation or context. They really represent or express the meaning of the Upaniṣads. Even among these statements there is conflict if we try to understand them rationally. However, as pointed out earlier, there can be no conflict among the different kinds of Upaniṣadic statements. Conflict is possible if all the Upaniṣadic statements have the same purpose in view or refer to the same reality. But there can be no conflict between the statements meant for instruction and the statements that deal with the objects of *upāsanā* and the statements that express the ontological vision or world-view of the Upaniṣads. They do not have the same kind of meaning and validity. Therefore, the problem of their reconciliation does not arise. But how to explain and reconcile the conflict among the basic or cardinal statements of the Upaniṣads? Can we say that the statements which express different views on creation are central to Upaniṣads? The problem of reconciliation arises mainly when we try to develop a coherent system of thought on the basis of statements that express the vision or world-view of the Upaniṣads, as well as the statements that express views on creation which are not compatible with each other. While in some statements *Brahman* is viewed as the cause or even as the creator of the world in some other statements any causal relationship is denied between *Brahman* and the world. Similar is the case with *Brahman* and *ātman*, and their relationship. Do we then find in the Upaniṣads any method to reconcile them?

Traditionally some of the Upaniṣadic statements are regarded as central or cardinal to understand the meaning of the Upaniṣads. They are central as they express clearly the world-view of the Upaniṣads. They are basic to understand the philosophy of the Upaniṣads. And among them the statement "all is *Brahman*" is more basic or fundamental, as without it the other cardinal Upaniṣadic statements will not be intelligible; they gain their meaning in terms of it. If *Brahman* is not present within all as their essence it would be futile to search for its presence within man, and the investigation into the nature of man would not be ontologically or spiritually significant. Then the Upaniṣads will have a different meaning and validity as the manner or mode of *Brahman*'s revelation will be different. The idea of the divine immanence is most central to understand the Upaniṣadic world-view, and without it the Upaniṣads will not be intelligible. All the Vedāntins are unanimous about its centrality to understand Vedānta, or one cannot be a Vedāntin without accepting the idea of divine immanence. This is fundamental to the world-view of the Upaniṣads, and it is more a matter of faith.

The vision that all that is there is *Brahman* or is permeated by *Brahman* gives rise to certain philosophical problems. In what sense the divine is present within all or what is the nature of the relationship between *Brahman* and all? Is *Brahman* different from all or are they not really different? If they are not really different what is the reality of all? These problems have exercised the minds of all the Vedāntins, and they differ among themselves in terms of their understanding of these problems. However, some of the Vedāntins are influenced in their understanding of the problems by their commitment to certain religious or theological beliefs and doctrines. Only a few have tried to understand the problems rationally and dispassionately. And one does not cease to be a Vedāntin in trying to understand the problems of Vedānta rationally. However, these problems are not the real concern of the Upaniṣads. They could, therefore, freely express various views on these problems without endorsing any one view or position. The Upaniṣads do not encourage us to be dogmatic in our approach to and understanding of such problems. But the vision that *Brahman* is immanently present within all is central to the Upaniṣadic world-view. The philosophical problems such as the nature of relationship between *Brahman*, and the world of empirical experience or between *Brahman* and *ātman* can be viewed in the light of the world-view but cannot be deducted logically from it. The Upaniṣadic statements like "all is *Brahman*" or "I am *Brahman*" are not metaphysical statements from which certain other statements can follow or be derived logically. These are matters of rational understanding with regard to which Upaniṣads have no authority, and therefore in not accepting any one view or position on such problems one does not cease to be a Vedāntin. One can be true to the Upaniṣads without accepting any view or position on such problems, or to be a Vedāntin it is not necessary to believe in any view or position on those problems. The meaningfulness or validity of any view or position in such matters depends upon its logical coherence as well as its harmony with the world-view of the Upaniṣads.

The above discussion naturally leads to the problem of the role and limits of logical reasoning in understanding such problems. There is one significant thing that is common to all those Vedāntins who oppose or reject the role of reason in understanding Vedānta. Although they vehemently deny any significant role to reason in understanding the meaning of Vedānta they employ it more vigorously in criticizing and rejecting the rival views and interpretations. And they feel justified in demolishing the rival positions on the basis of logical reasoning even though they vehemently deny any significant role to reason as far as their positions or views are concerned.

What could be the role of reason in understanding the problem of relationship between *Brahman* and the world of empirical experience, or between *Brahman* and *ātman*? Right from Bādarāyaṇa to Sri Aurobindo we find a positive attitude towards reason in understanding such problems though they have their own problems in determining its role and limits. Here we have to make a clear and fine distinction. It is one thing to take the help of reason in knowing or understanding the divine and its nature, and quite another to depend upon it in resolving the problem of reconciliation between the divine and the world. If all that is there is *Brahman* what could be the relationship between *Brahman* and all, or to put it in the context of the Upaniṣads how to reconcile the Upaniṣadic statements in which *Brahman* is viewed as the source or cause of the world of empirical experience, and the statements in which any relationship is denied between *Brahman* and the world. In some of the Upaniṣadic texts the world is seen as a spontaneous self-expression of *Brahman* or its nature, like sparks emanating from fire, or a spider weaving a web, or growth of hair from the body of a living person.[2] The manifestation or expression of the world on the part of *Brahman* is as spontaneous and natural like the process of breathing in and breathing out in all living beings. However, in some of the Upaniṣads the existence of the world is seen as due to the will of *Brahman* (God). He wished or wanted to create, and so He created the world out of Himself. He created the world, and entered Himself into it unto the last detail. As a spontaneous self-expression or as an expression of divine creativity (*kāvya*) the world is not created in the ordinary sense. It is co-eternal as well as co-extensive with *Brahman*. Thus, it is in a logical sense only the world depends for its existence on *Brahman* as the idea or existence of *Brahman* is logically prior to that of the world. The Upaniṣads even identify creation with *Brahman*.[3]

Similar is the case with *Brahman* in the Upaniṣads. While in several Upaniṣadic texts something positive is said about *Brahman*, in some other statements all that is said about *Brahman* is denied. *Brahman* is not what we meditate upon or worship. There exists nothing besides *Brahman*; it is one without a second. Now, in what sense can reason help us in reconciling such mutually conflicting statements found in the Upaniṣads either about *Brahman* or about the relationship between *Brahman* and the world of empirical experience. All the

2. *Muṇḍaka Upaniṣad* 1.1.7; see also *Bṛhadāraṇyaka Upaniṣad* 2.1.20.
3. *Bṛhadāraṇyaka Upaniṣad*. 1.4.5.

statements cannot be equally authoritative and valid. If one kind of statements are true the other kind of statements cannot be true, or if we give validity to one kind of statements we have to deny validity to other kind of statements. We have then to explain the significance and status of the statements which cannot be regarded as valid and authoritative. The problem can be formulated differently. Instead of trying to find out their consistency on logical grounds we can try to analyse and understand the concepts involved, and see whether they can be logically related. The Buddhist philosophers had adopted this method before Śaṅkara. The concepts of *Brahman* and world do not belong to the same level or genre. While *Brahman* is not an empirically meaningful concept, the world is an empirically meaningful concept. While the one is based on empirical experience, the other is not. Therefore, our analysis and understanding of both the concepts cannot be done at the same level as they are not amenable to the same logic. We cannot apply the same logic to them. Although the concept of *Brahman* is in a sense based on experience as it is conceived to be present within what is empirically experienced, yet as it is not identical with anything that is empirically experienced we have to admit a transcendental dimension to it. And in its transcendental dimension it is not intelligible in terms of our rational understanding and its categories which are meaningful and valid within the empirical sphere. Furthermore, we cannot but think of *Brahman* as perfect being or as perfection itself (*pūrṇa*), and the idea of perfection is not compatible with certain ideas. More importantly, the idea of perfection is not amenable to empirical analysis and understanding as nothing positive can be said about it that is empirically meaningful. If by definition *Brahman* is absolute perfection, and eternally self-fulfilled there can be no reason why it should act or be a cause. Causation is an empirical category, and meaningful within the realm of empirical experience. It involves the idea of purpose or some kind of reason, and they presuppose lack of perfection on the part of cause. Any purpose or motive on the part of *Brahman* in creating the world goes against its perfection. Causation of any type involves purpose or motive on the part of *Brahman*, and purpose or motive is not consistent with the idea of perfection. And if *Brahman* is regarded as the sole cause of the world then the idea of cause involves change or mutation in the nature of *Brahman*. Without some kind of change in its nature *Brahman* cannot become the cause of the world. On the other hand, if the world is regarded as a spontaneous self-manifestation of *Brahman* it cannot be viewed as having a beginning. Then the world cannot also be regarded as substantially different from *Brahman*. As a self-expression or manifestation of *Brahman* the world comes into existence as spontaneously or naturally as the breathing process in man. Similarly, the idea of world when analysed does not involve the idea of effect. The world is not an artefact, nor has it a beginning in time as the ultimate components or the basic elements that constitute the world do not point to a cause; they exist by themselves. They are not caused to exist. They are ultimately real.

As the idea of cause is not compatible with the idea of *Brahman* all the attempts to explain the world in terms of *Brahman* end in contradictions. Nevertheless, the Upaniṣads talk of *Brahman* and world, and the Upaniṣadic statements about *Brahman* and world are not really reconcilable. In this regard we have to appreciate the philosophical position of Śaṅkara. According to him the problem of reconciliation arises when one applies the same logic to understand both kinds of Upaniṣadic statements. What is empirically meaningful and valid may not be so transcendentally, and vice versa. Similarly what is practically or existentially meaningful and valid need not be so objectively, and vice versa. Now, a religious or practical way of understanding the problem of reconciliation may be more meaningful and valid, but it does not mean that it should be ontologically valid or objectively true. The Upaniṣads are not authority or proof for the objective validity of any religious view or belief as they contain several such views, and all of them cannot be true even if they are found in the Upaniṣads. Practical or pragmatic or existential validity is one thing and ontological or objective validity is another. While the religious or theological beliefs have practical or pragmatic validity, the ontological validity of a belief or view depends on the authority of Śruti and direct experience. Therefore, all the views expressed in the Upaniṣads cannot have ontological validity, and for that reason we cannot deny ontological validity to all the Upaniṣadic statements. In other words, we cannot justify a religious view on the authority of the Upaniṣads, nor can such views, even when they find a place in the Upaniṣads, be reconciled with the idea of *Brahman* or the world-view of the Upaniṣads. And there can be no Upaniṣadic justification or authority to define *Brahman* in such a way as to make it compatible with certain religious or theological views and beliefs. On the other hand, trying to find compatibility between the ontological vision of the Upaniṣads and a theological doctrine or position is to misunderstand the nature of both, and consequently deny meaningfulness and validity to one or the other.

Now, how to explain the fact that the Upaniṣads not only represent a world-view or an ontological vision but also express certain theological beliefs and doctrines. The latter cannot have any logical relationship with the former. But as they find expression in the Upaniṣads they cannot be rejected as having only a practical value and validity. If *Brahman* cannot be the explanation of the world, and yet the world appears to be real as all the theological views refer to the reality of the world, how to explain its reality and reconcile it with that of *Brahman*? The concept or rather the category of *māyā* is introduced by Śaṅkara at this point in the philosophical development of Vedānta. It stands for or points to two things. Firstly, the problem of reconciliation can have no satisfactory or adequate metaphysical solution, and secondly the enigmatic character of the world. The concept or category of *māyā* eludes rational or metaphysical understanding and explanation, just as the problem of reconciliation between *Brahman* and world eludes logical or philosophical understanding. No explanation of it can be logically coherent or there can be no logically coherent explanation of it. In the final analysis, *māyā* stands to mean or points to the limits of human reason in understanding and resolving the problem of reconciliation between the two kinds of Upaniṣadic statements, or in explaining the relationship between *Brahman* and the world. Though *Brahman* is immanent in the world yet it transcends the world. It has a transcendental dimension which is not amenable to rational understanding of man which is guided by the categories developed on the basis of man's empirical experience. Therefore, rational understanding of man cannot fully comprehend the divine and its nature. However, when it tries to understand and determine the nature of *Brahman* as well as its relationship with the world of empirical experience several logical problems arise which it cannot resolve. The failure of reason to comprehend the nature of *Brahman* as well as its inability to explain the relationship between *Brahman* and the world is indicated by the category of *māyā*.

In any attempt to rationally understand the Upaniṣads or to develop a rationally coherent philosophy of the Upaniṣads one has to face the problem of reconciliation between *Brahman* and the world of empirical experience or between the two kinds of Upaniṣadic statements. This has been the major problem faced by almost all the interpreters of Vedānta. According to Śaṅkara, the problem of reconciliation eludes human understanding as it has no rational solution. Instead of admitting the limits of human reason in understanding and resolving the problem of reconciliation, if we try to define *Brahman* in such a manner as to make it lend support, or provide justification to a theological doctrine or position then the Upaniṣads lose their identity and authority, as in that case they can be made to lend their authority to any theological view or position.

The problem can be viewed in another way. If *Brahman* is the only reality that exists or it is one without a second then it should be regarded as the explanation of everything other than itself, including the metaphysical or theological views and beliefs that have no ontological validity. If we consider that the theological views and doctrines have only pragmatic or practical validity, for they are the creation of human imagination, we have to explain such imagination ultimately in terms of *Brahman*. We have to remember in this connection that though the Upaniṣads recognize the importance of all the human faculties in knowing truth, the truth revealed in the Upaniṣads is not due to human capacity to know or understand. *Brahman* of the Upaniṣads is not the absolute of speculative metaphysics. It is not a postulate of speculative reason to explain the world. *Brahman* is known or realized directly and immediately as that which is immanently present within all, including man. Thus, even if we fail to explain the world of empirical experience in terms of *Brahman* the reality of *Brahman* cannot be denied. The Upaniṣadic *Brahman* is not an idea or concept postulated to explain the world. It is that which inspires in man speech or wisdom, devotion and prayer whereby man's life is supremely fulfilled. The *Brahman* of the Upaniṣads cannot be equated with the absolute of speculative metaphysics. While *Brahman* of the Upaniṣads is self-evident as it is the being or self of man, the absolute requires proof for its existence. It can be denied when we cannot prove its existence, but to deny existence to *Brahman* of the Upaniṣads is to presuppose its existence. However, Bādarāyaṇa starts his *Brahma-Sūtras* with a proof for the existence of *Brahman*, *janmādyasya yataḥ*.[4] If *Brahman* depends for its existence on proofs or arguments it can also be proved not to exist. If certain proofs can be devised to prove its existence equally powerful arguments can be invented to disprove its existence. But the *Brahman* of the Upaniṣads is not a matter of rational understanding and proof as they talk of *Brahman* that is known or experienced directly and immediately.

Of course, the Upaniṣads also speak of *Brahman* which is the explanation of the world. In several views on creation

4. *Brahma-Sūtras*, 1.1.2.

expressed in the Upaniṣads *Brahman* is regarded as the creator or cause of the world. *Brahman* is conceived as that by knowing which everything else is known.[5] Such views on *Brahman* expressed in the Upaniṣads are the basis for several interpreters to explain the world in terms of *Brahman*, or *Brahman* as the ultimate source or cause of the world. However, such views expressed in the Upaniṣads need not be regarded as representing the truth of the Upaniṣads, or as having ontological validity, for all such views are negated by the Upaniṣads themselves. The two kinds of statements found in the Upaniṣads cannot be regarded as equally important and authoritative in understanding the vision or world-view of the Upaniṣads, as in that case it would not be possible to know or understand the meaning of the Upaniṣads or its world-view. If we think that both kinds of statements are true to the Upaniṣads, and represent their wisdom we have to admit that the Upaniṣads do not have a focus or unity of thought. They are then to be viewed as a collection of views without a vision of their own, and in that case it would be futile to think of a philosophy of the Upaniṣads. On the other hand, if we try to deny validity to some of the Upaniṣadic statements, like the statements on creation, as they are not compatible with other kinds of statements we have to explain their place and significance in the Upaniṣads. How to understand and explain the presence of mutually conflicting views in the Upaniṣads? And more importantly how to reconcile the statements which do not seem to represent the Upaniṣads with those that are considered as representative of the wisdom or world-view of the Upaniṣads? In other words, we have to explain the presence in the Upaniṣads of two kinds of statements which are in conflict with each other, and even negate each other.

Another important aspect of Śaṅkara's approach to Vedānta is that if one is justified in analysing and criticizing the rival views on the basis of reason there can be no justification for exempting one's own view or position from rational analysis

5. *Muṇḍaka Upaniṣad* 1.1.3 (*yad jñātvā saramidaṁ vijñātaṁ bhavati*).

and criticism. The fact that reason cannot know *Brahman* does not mean that it cannot point out the contradictions and other kinds of logical fallacies in one's thought and in the thought of others as well. If the metaphysical positions of rival schools, like Sāṁkhya and Buddhism, can be rationally understood and criticized there is no valid reason to withhold reason from understanding and criticizing the metaphysical positions or doctrines of the Vedāntins. Almost all the doctrines and even theologies developed by different Vedāntins are in reality based on rational understanding though some kind of Upaniṣadic authority is adduced in support or justification of them mainly to claim for their interpretations immunity from rational criticism. Such interpretations of the Upaniṣads or Vedānta are valid from a narrow technical point of view as they can adduce some of the Upaniṣadic statements in justification of their views. But they do not take into consideration all the Upaniṣadic texts or statements, or a total or comprehensive view or understanding of the Upaniṣads, or their vision or world-view, in understanding the philosophy of the Upaniṣads, but depend upon some of the statements that apparently lend support or authority to their interpretation. Such interpretations seem to be true to the Upaniṣads as they also depend on the authority of the Upaniṣads. However, as such interpretations are meant to justify a theological belief or doctrine they have a religious or emotional appeal. More importantly they try to avoid or even explain away the problem of reconciliation between the two kinds of Upaniṣadic statements or the conflict between the two kinds of statements which is crucial in developing a philosophy of Vedānta.

In this connection we have to make a distinction between *Brahman*, which is a matter of direct experience or realization, and the various views and doctrines developed supposedly on the basis of it. We cannot admit that the various views or doctrines developed on the basis of the Upaniṣads enjoy the same status and validity of the Upaniṣads. Here again it is reason that can point out the fact that the various views and doctrines developed by different philosophers do not follow logically from what is said in the Upaniṣads or from any Upaniṣadic statement. On the other hand, if it is maintained that a particular interpretation is based on all the texts and statements of the Upaniṣads then that interpretation has to face the problem of reconciliation between the two kinds of Upaniṣadic statements. Therefore, no system of Vedānta can claim for itself the authority and validity of the Upaniṣads, and consequently immunity from rational analysis and criticism. The doctrines or theories developed to reconcile the two kinds of Upaniṣadic statements or to explain the reality of the world in terms of *Brahman* are not beyond the purview of reason as reason plays a significant role in their development. They can therefore be analysed, criticized and even rejected without thereby denying validity to the Upaniṣads.

Furthermore, there is no sufficient justification for determining the meaning of the Upaniṣadic statements in terms of a doctrine. In the face of different systems of Vedānta or different doctrines about the relationship between *Brahman* and the world we cannot say that all or anyone of them is true to the Upaniṣads. The only way to decide the validity of any doctrine is to understand whether it can follow logically from the Upaniṣads or is it compatible with the nature of *Brahman* as revealed in the Upaniṣads. If any doctrine on creation cannot be deduced logically from the Upaniṣadic statements, and if the concept of *Brahman* is not compatible with the concept of creation then the doctrines in which *Brahman* is viewed as the ultimate cause or explanation of the world cannot be regarded as true to the spirit of the Upaniṣads. The Upaniṣadic *Brahman* is not a metaphysical notion or concept from which other concepts can be logically derived or around which a system of metaphysics can be developed.

Another important contribution of Śaṅkara to Vedānta is that as long as we are in the realm of empirical reality or experience, and try to understand *Brahman* from an empirical point of view *Brahman* remains an idea meant to explain the world process. As a metaphysical principle or idea its validity depends upon its capacity to explain the world process adequately. In this process what is empirically meaningful or significant is attributed to *Brahman*, and *Brahman* is sought to be understood in terms of categories of understanding which are derived from empirical experience, and are valid in relation to it. There can be no rational justification for understanding and defining what is not empirically real in terms of the categories whose significance and validity are limited to the realm of empirical experience. And if *Brahman* is amenable to logic based on empirical experience and its categories then to distinguish it from the world of empirical experience would be meaningless and futile. *Brahman* must then be viewed as an object of empirical experience or as forming part of empirical reality. In that case to think of *Brahman* as the cause of the world of empirical experience will be unintelligible as it is itself a part of the empirical world. On the other hand, if we admit that the reality of *Brahman* transcends empirical understanding and its categories then we cannot say anything about *Brahman* in empirically meaningful terms. In other words, *Brahman* is as good as *śūnya* in relation to our empirical understanding and its categories.

Brahman as consciousness is immanent in human experience and transcends it as well. We cannot say anything about consciousness as its reality is presupposed by all such statements or assertions. It cannot be an object of a statement either empirical or scriptural. *Brahman* as pure consciousness is real and objective though it is not an object of any knowledge or experience. It cannot therefore be expressed in a language which is empirically meaningful. The consciousness which is known at the empirical level as the reality or self of man is also the reality of all that is there is a matter of revelation or world-view for which we have to depend upon the Upaniṣads. The world-view or the ontological vision of the Upaniṣads is not a matter of rational understanding nor is it based on any mystical experience. Therefore, the doctrines, either metaphysical or theological, supposedly based on or inspired by the world-view or are developed on the basis of it need not be logically valid as we cannot establish any logical connection between the two. We cannot also relate logically the world-view with any doctrine or theology as it is not possible to logically deduce any doctrine from the world-view. But the doctrines or theologies may seem to be meaningful to those for whom the world-view is meaningful despite the fact that they are not logically related. The world-view is meaningful by itself which is not, however, the case with the doctrines supposedly based on it. All rational justification in support of the world-view is really futile as its meaningfulness does not depend upon reason, or on its rationality. Therefore, to accept the Upaniṣads is to accept a vision or a world-view, but not any doctrine or a system of doctrines. The world-view gives meaning to the world and life. But as the world-view cannot, logically speaking, be the source of any doctrine or theology we cannot justify any doctrine or theology on the basis of a world-view.

The object of Śaṅkara in interpreting the Upaniṣads or Vedānta is to make us grasp and realize the world-view of the Upaniṣads, but not to make us accept or believe in any doctrine or theology in the name of the Upaniṣads. And as reason plays an important role in the development of various Vedāntic doctrines their validity should be judged in terms of reason. The metaphysical doctrines whether they belong to rival schools or are developed on the basis or authority of the Upaniṣads depend for their coherence and validity on the rational understanding of man. Although most of the Vedāntins vehemently oppose the role of reason in their interpretation of Vedānta openly they accept it in practice when they criticize the views of others and provide justification for their views as well as to defend them from the criticism of others.

5

Abhinavagupta

ALTHOUGH Kashmir Śaivism, also known as Pratyabhijñā or Śaivādvaita, is not a school of Vedānta it is nevertheless relevant and helpful in understanding the philosophical development of Vedānta. Among the non-Vedānta Schools of Indian philosophy it made a serious attempt to understand the problem of reconciliation between the absolute and the world of empirical experience. As discussed in the previous chapters the problem of reconciliation between *Brahman* and the world or between the two kinds of Upaniṣadic statements has been felt and discussed by almost all the Vedāntins though they differ in their approaches to the problem.

The Upaniṣads are a major source of inspiration to almost all the sects of Hinduism even though they are not Upaniṣadic in origin. In their theological development they are deeply influenced by the Upaniṣads as each major sect of Hinduism has in its own way tried to adapt the Upaniṣadic or Vedāntic ontology in understanding and defining the nature of the deity around which the sects are formed and developed. Almost all the Vedāntins, who came after Śaṅkara, have tried to adapt Vedānta, particularly its ontology, to their sectarian theologies with a view to providing them ontological basis and justification as well as to make them appear Śruti based, or to give the authority of Śruti to them. Their intention in interpreting the Vedānta is not so much to develop a philosophy of Vedānta, but to adapt it to their sectarian theological needs. In their attempts to adapt the Upaniṣadic ontology to serve the sectarian theological needs the great Vedāntins who came after

Śaṅkara unwittingly helped the philosophical development of Vedānta though they have added in the process a theological or religious dimension to Vedānta. Thereby they helped in bringing Vedānta closer to people or made it more meaningful or intelligible to popular understanding. The author of the *Brahma-Sūtras* and Śaṅkara are philosophical in their understanding of the Upaniṣads, and had no intention of utilizing the Upaniṣads to serve any religious or theological purpose. We do not find in their interpretations, particularly that of Śaṅkara, any attempt to support or justify any theological or metaphysical position. They tried to follow the logic internal to a theological or metaphysical position or to any possible Vedāntic position to its logical end, just as they did in trying to understand and criticize rival philosophical views or positions. In other words, they tried to follow the logic of an argument either of their opponents or of their own to its logical end as they have realized that the real object of the Upaniṣads is to express or communicate something that transcends rational understanding of man. The Upaniṣads are the ultimate authority and justification for Vedānta, and they really stand for an ontological vision or world-view. Therefore, the object of Bādarāyaṇa and Śaṅkara in interpreting the Upaniṣads is to uphold the world-view of the Upaniṣads, and defend it against the criticisms of rival schools or systems of philosophy. They followed reason in understanding and criticizing the rival views and doctrines as well as in defending Vedānta from the criticisms of rival schools. However, they have not tried to support or justify, in terms of reason, any theological or metaphysical position or doctrine purported to be of the Upaniṣads. The ontological vision or world-view of the Upaniṣads is ultimately a matter of faith and personal realization. It does not stand in need of rational support or justification as its meaning cannot be defined or determined in terms of any metaphysical or theological doctrine.

It is a different problem whether the vision or world-view of the Upaniṣads is the same as, or at least similar to, the vision of God as defined or described in different sectarian theologies of Hinduism, like that of Śaivism or Vaiṣṇavism. Can *Brahman* of the Upaniṣads, often referred to as That, be identified with Śiva or Viṣṇu or Śakti? Can the sectarian deities of Hinduism like Śiva or Viṣṇu be identified with *Brahman* of the Upaniṣads?

The Kashmir Śaivism is developed on the basis of the *Śiva-sūtras* which is in a sense revealed, though not in the Vedic sense, and enjoy the status and authority of revelation as far as Kashmir Śaivism is concerned. Although Kashmir Śaivism is not strictly speaking a school of Vedānta, its major thinkers are well acquainted with Vedānta and its ontology as well as the problem of reconciliation between *Brahman* and the world or between the absolute and the phenomenal world. In their attempts to identify the sectarian deities like Śiva and Viṣṇu with the *Brahman* of the Upaniṣads the theologians of different Hindu sects have recognized the importance of the problem of reconciliation between the absolute and the phenomenal. In other words, in the process of identifying the sectarian deities with the *Brahman* of the Upaniṣads the theologians of different sects have faced the problem of explaining the world process in terms of Śiva or Viṣṇu identified as *Brahman*. It is one thing to religiously believe in the personal character of God, whose will or desire is sufficient to create the world or bring it into existence, and quite another to understand the world process in terms of *Brahman* which transcends the categories of human understanding, including religious or theological. Furthermore, how to justify the identification of the various sectarian deities with *Brahman* without compromising the personal character and religious significance of the deities? The Upaniṣadic *Brahman* is not personal, or rather it is beyond the categories of personal and impersonal. But unless it is interpreted to have a personal dimension its religious value and significance cannot be appreciated by people. It cannot become an object of religious devotion and worship.

Kashmir Śaivism, which is primarily a religious tradition, has tried to adapt the Vedāntic ontology in developing its theology centred round the deity of Śiva. In its attempts to adapt Vedānta to Śaivism, it tries to make a subtle or fine distinction between Śiva and Parama-Śiva. Although Parama-Śiva is not in reality different from Śiva, conceptually Parama-Śiva transcends the concept of Śiva. Similarly, Parama-Śiva transcends the world though he is conceived to be present in the world, or the world is seen as his manifestation. His nature cannot, therefore, be understood and defined in terms of theological or metaphysical categories; He transcends them. In a sense Parama-Śiva is comparable to *Brahman* of the Upaniṣads, and the thinkers of Kashmir Śaivism try to identify Parama-Śiva more with the *Brahman* of Advaita than with that of the Upaniṣads. Now the basic problem faced by the theologians of Kashmir Śaivism is how to understand and explain the distinction between Parama-Śiva and Śiva, or how to explain the emergence of Śiva from Parama-Śiva. While it is religiously significant to explain the world as a creation of Śiva, it is not so in terms of Parama-Śiva. Although Parama-Śiva is not directly involved in the creation of the world yet he is related to it in the form of Śiva, its creator. As the nature of Parama-Śiva is conceived in absolute terms he cannot be the explanation of the world as it involves causation on the part of Parama-Śiva, which is not compatible with his absolute character. But then how to explain the reality of Śiva, the creator of the world, in terms of Parama-Śiva, or how to reconcile the theistic concept of Śiva with the *Brahman* of Vedānta identified as Parama-Śiva? Is it possible to reconcile the concepts of Śiva and Parama-Śiva without giving up the theistic character of Śiva and the absolute character of Parama-Śiva? While there is no problem of explaining the world in terms of the theistic concept of Śiva, the concept of Parama-Śiva cannot be reconciled with the idea of creation. Parama-Śiva cannot be the explanation of the world process as we cannot attribute to Parama-Śiva any kind of causation without compromising his absolute character and perfection. This is similar to the problem of reconciliation between *Brahman* and the world faced by the Vedāntins. However, Kashmir Śaivism tries to resolve the problem of reconciliation between Parama-Śiva and Śiva in terms of *spanda*, a creative and dynamic principle which is inherent in the nature of Parama-Śiva.

Kashmir Śaivism introduces the concept or principle of *spanda* in order to explain the reality of the world process without compromising at the same time the absolute perfection of Parama-Śiva. *Spanda* is conceived as something that is intrinsic to the nature of Parama-Śiva. It is a creative principle in terms of which Parama-Śiva is self-conscious as well as the power of His self-expression or manifestation. In other words, it is because of *spanda* Parama-Śiva who is pure consciousness is also known as self-consciousness. According to Kashmir Śaivism, there is no antagonism or conflict between pure consciousness and self-consciousness as Parama-Śiva is both. Parama-Śiva who is pure consciousness, and one without a second is ever conscious of himself because of *spanda*. He is eternally self-conscious or self-consciousness is intrinsic to his nature (*prakāśa vimarṣamaya*).[1] He is eternally an experient

---

1. Although this chapter deals with the problem of reconciliation between the absolute and the phenomenal as understood and discussed in the Kashmir Śaivism, it is named after Abhinavagupta, a representative thinker of Kashmir Śaivism. The chapter is not on Abhinavagupta and his philosophy; it is on Kashmir Śaivism. However, keeping in view the theme of the book and the titles of other chapters this chapter is named after Abhinavagupta.

   In Kashmir Śaivism the nature of Parama-Śiva or the ultimate reality is conceived in dynamic terms. He is pure consciousness which is at the same time self-consciousness because the power whereby Parama-Śiva knows himself and manifests himself is intrinsic to his nature, just as the power to grow itself into a huge tree is inherently present in the seed of a banyan tree. Without the power to manifest himself or without the power of self-consciousness (*śakti*) Śiva would be as good as dead. Thus, Parama-Śiva is both light of consciousness as well as the power to know himself and manifest himself (*prakāśa-vimarśamaya*). *Śiva-Sūtras* Introduction, pages xx and xxi. In the concept or person of Parama-Śiva both Śiva and Śakti are integrated. They are inseparable within the person of Parama-Śiva.

→

whether there is something other than himself which can be an object of his experience or not. In other words, though he transcends subject-object distinction or duality he is never without his self-awareness. He is pure subject even though there exists nothing other than himself which can be an object of his renience. Thus the major contention of Kashmir Śaivism is that pure consciousness is at the same time self-consciousness, and there is no opposition between them.

In terms of the creative power or *spanda* which is intrinsic to his nature Parama-Śiva manifests himself, and as an expression of his nature the different forms of his manifestation or the world is not really different from himself. In reality, Parama-Śiva is not different from his self-expression or manifestation though they may appear to be so to an unenlightened person. Parama-Śiva and the varied forms of his self-expression or manifestation are not different from each other as one cannot exist without the other. They are not two, or non-dual. In this sense Kashmir Śaivism is Advaita (Śiva-advaita) as it identifies Parama-Śiva with *Brahman* or the absolute. Parama-Śiva in the state of his manifestation is known as Śiva, and therefore transcends Śiva. Parama-Śiva is the transcendental aspect of Śiva. The distinction made between Parama-Śiva and Śiva is similar to the distinction made between *Brahman* and *Īśvara* in Vedānta. Thus, a significant attempt is made in Kashmir Śaivism to identify or equate Parama-Śiva of Śaivism with *Brahman* of Vedānta. While in his transcendental state Śiva is known as Parama-Śiva, Parama-Śiva is known as Śiva in the state of his self-expression or manifestation. In other words, Śiva and Śakti are integrated in the concept of Parama-Śiva.

Kashmir Śaivism is also the first to attempt reconciliation between the Smṛti and Śruti traditions, or more specifically

---

→ "The divine is termed the great lord (Maheśvara) because of his ever-present immutable self-awareness (*vimarśa*). That self-awareness in its absolute freedom constitutes divine knowledge and activity." *sa eva vimṛśatvena niyatena maheśvarah, vimarśa eva devasya śuddhe jñānikriye yataḥ* — *Īśvarapratyabhijñā* 1.8.11.

between the Upaniṣads and Śaivism without rejecting or denying the basic or essential characteristics of either. In its attempts to reconcile Śaivism with Vedānta Kashmir Śaivism has neither rejected the non-dual and absolute character of *Brahman* nor the theistic character of Śaivism. Instead it tried to conceive and define Śiva in Advaitic terms. Śiva is seen as having a transcendental dimension which is beyond the categories of human understanding including religious or theological. In his transcendental aspect Śiva is known as Parama-Śiva. And Parama-Śiva is a self-conscious being in whom the power to manifest or express himself is inherent. As the power to manifest himself is intrinsic to his nature his manifestation of himself in the form of world is not a sign of imperfection. The absolute is conceived in dynamic terms so that the existence of the world need not be viewed as an act on the part of the absolute. Self-manifestation on the part of Parama-Śiva is spontaneous as the power to manifest himself is intrinsic to his nature. Therefore, it is not due to any motive or imperfection that Parama-Śiva manifests himself. It is his nature to manifest himself, and therefore Parama-Śiva and his manifestation or the world are equally real. But they are not different as one cannot exist without the other. We cannot also understand them separately as neither can exist independently of the other. The world as self-manifestation of Parama-Śiva is substantially not different from him, and because of his dynamic nature Parama-Śiva cannot remain static or without his self-expression. One is essential to the other. Both are inseparable, and yet they are one in the person of Parama-Śiva. Thus, Kashmir Śaivism tries to prove the reality of the world without compromising on the non-dual and absolute character of Śiva in terms of its conception of Parama-Śiva in whose person Śiva and Śakti are integrated. Parama-Śiva who is pure consciousness is at the same time self-consciousness.

We will now try to understand whether the explanation of Kashmir Śaivism is philosophically adequate and meaningful. The absolute or Parama-Śiva in creating the world does not act in response to any external demand or due to any internal urge or desire. He manifests himself in the form of the world due to creativity which is his nature. He is, therefore, completely autonomous in creating the world. According to Kashmir Śaivism, pure consciousness without being self-consciousness will be as good as a dead or inert principle or reality, like a self-shining crystal or light. Consciousness to be meaningful must be selfconsciousness. "People know *vimarśa*, the very nature of the light of consciousness; otherwise like light even when reflecting things consciousness would be insentient like a crystal."[2] Consciousness, without being self-conscious, will be as good as insentient, and even non-existent, because it will then be devoid of the power to express or manifest itself. A reality which does not manifest itself in any form is as good as non-existent as it cannot make itself known. We know consciousness only when it manifests itself, and that power to manifest itself is intrinsic to itself. Otherwise consciousness cannot manifest or reveal itself.

Because of the creative power inherent within itself the absolute becomes the "other" as it were, or the absolute which is pure subject manifests as "the other," the object. Thus, the subject-object duality emerges, and the world process starts. The world process is, therefore, not due to another reality which is different from or other than Parama-Śiva, or due to any influence, either external or internal, on Parama-Śiva. As the principle of *spanda* is intrinsic to Parama-Śiva the process of world manifestation is spontaneous on the part of Parama-Śiva. The world process is not due to any desire or motive on the part of Parama-Śiva, or there is no reason or explanation of any kind for the world to come into existence. It is the nature of Parama-Śiva to manifest himself because of *spanda śakti* that is inherent within himself. It may thus appear that Kashmir Śaivism or Śaivādvaita could offer a meaningful and philosophically adequate solution to the problem of reconciliation between *Brahman* and the world, or between the absolute and the phenomenal, or the two kinds of Vedānta

2. *Īśvarapratyabhijñā* 1.5.11.

statements without denying reality to what is empirically experienced. Both are real, and yet they are not different from each other. They are not two because the world as a spontaneous self-manifestation of Parama-Śiva is not different from him. And for the same reason, the world in any manner does not limit or condition Parama-Śiva. It is the manifestation of his nature, and being a manifestation of his own nature the world process does not in any manner bind Parama-Śiva nor does its reality mean or imply any kind of limitation or imperfection in the nature of Parama-Śiva. The world is a free and creative manifestation of his nature though it may appear as if it is other than and different from Parama-Śiva.

The above explanation in which Kashmir Śaivism tries to maintain the reality of the world as well as the transcendent and absolute character of Parama-Śiva may satisfy the theological needs of Śaivism, but leaves the problem of reconciliation between the absolute and the phenomenal or between *Brahman* and the world unresolved philosophically. We take up for discussion two problems which are basic to the position of Kashmir Śaivism. Firstly, what is it for consciousness to manifest itself, and secondly how in the absence of a reality other than himself Parama-Śiva can be regarded as a self-conscious being or as an eternal experient? Kashmir Śaivism identifies Parama-Śiva with pure consciousness, but as having the power or capacity to manifest himself. It regards pure consciousness or *Brahman* of Advaita as pure light without the dynamism required to manifest or reveal itself. It is, therefore, as good as an inert reality though self-refulgent. But how far the analogy of light can help us in understanding the nature of consciousness? The analogy of light to understand the nature of consciousness will be misleading because light is a physical reality to which awareness in any form cannot be attributed. However, the analogy is appropriate in one respect, that is, pure consciousness is like pure light as it does not depend upon another principle for its revelation, just as light does not depend upon another light for its illumination. Consciousness is self-evident as light is self-shining. But how to understand and decide whether consciousness, that is, *Brahman* is devoid of self-awareness? Light which illuminates objects also illuminates itself simultaneously, or its illumination of itself is simultaneous with the objects it illumines. But to be known or to be revealed, light as a physical reality, depends upon consciousness which however is not the case with consciousness. The analogy between consciousness and light is meaningful and relevant to the extent that both are self-revealing or self-illuminating. But consciousness is not a physical reality so as to depend upon another reality for its knowledge or revelation. A simple but highly significant parable of Sri Ramakrishna will be of help in grasping the meaning of pure consciousness. He once asked his disciples as to what they would do or how would they enjoy if nectar was offered to them, and if they were to be bees. Many have said that they would like to sit around the nectar and sip it, whereas Vivekānanda said that he would jump into it.[3] Then the other disciples wondered whether Vivekānanda would not be drowned in nectar. It is a case of analogy in which empirical experience of death by drowning is extended to understand the meaning of drowning in nectar, which is deathlessness. In the case of nectar drowning does not mean death as it is immortality or deathlessness. Similarly, to think that pure consciousness is devoid of self-awareness or is not conscious of itself is to stretch or extend the empirical experience and its categories to what transcends empirical experience. Light which can illuminate things as well as itself is not conscious of itself as it is a physical reality. Can we say meaningfully that in the absence of objects to be illuminated light will illuminate itself? It is superfluous to assert that light illuminates itself in the absence of objects to illuminate as it is light, and its nature to illuminate is never lost. Here we may consider another example. We know fire as that which burns things. Can we then say that in the absence of objects to burn fire burns itself, or does not exist when it does not burn? We

3. See *The Gospel of Ramakrishna*.

come to know of fire only when it burns objects, and when it does not burn objects we do not know about it as it does not manifest itself. Similarly, to think that Parama-Śiva, who is pure consciousness, is not conscious of himself amounts to saying that pure consciousness is not consciousness. Now, the Kashmir Śaivism may point out that to be aware of is not the same as self-consciousness which a person has of himself. The consciousness of oneself as expressed in "I am" (*aham*), or I-consciousness is not the same as simple awareness or consciousness. However, pure consciousness which is free from subject-object distinction, or rather transcends subject-object distinction cannot be regarded as self-consciousness because there is no reality other than consciousness in relation to which it can become self-conscious. I-consciousness involves object-consciousness, whatever may be the nature of the object, be it an idea or a physical object. At the level of empirical experience one becomes self-conscious in relation to his consciousness of an object, be it mental or physical. Self-consciousness and object-consciousness go together, or they are two aspects or sides of the same experience. Both are involved in any kind of experience at the empirical level as one is not intelligible without the other. During subjective state of consciousness one is conscious of his mental states, and in the objective state of consciousness one is conscious of physical objects. And in the absence of an object of experience, physical or mental, one is not known as a subject. At the empirical level, consciousness flows as it were towards an object, and in the process it becomes aware of itself. To know or to be aware of at the empirical level means to know or to be conscious of something, because the transitive verb "to know" points to an object that is to be known, like the verb "to cut" points to an object that is to be cut. In the absence of an object to know "knowing" will not be meaningful, just as cutting will not be meaningful without an object to cut. Thus, "to know" or "to be conscious" is not intelligible without an object to be known or to be conscious of. And a person is known as a knower or a subject only when he knows something, but not otherwise. Similarly, one is said to be self-conscious only when he is conscious of some object. In other words, self-consciousness is meaningful only in relation to object-consciousness. Self-consciousness and object-consciousness are two aspects or sides of an experience at the empirical level, and therefore in the absence of one or the other experience at the empirical level is not possible. In the light of the above analysis we can say that self-consciousness is not meaningful in the absence of object-consciousness as self-awareness and object-awareness depend upon each other.

Now it may be pointed out that in the case of Parama-Śiva his self-consciousness is not in relation to his awareness of something other than himself. His self-consciousness is in relation to himself, and all that he is potentially or all that is inherent within himself. He is conscious of himself or his being as potentially containing the world. Parama-Śiva is self-conscious in the sense he is ever conscious of his possibilities, or he experiences himself eternally in the sense he is conscious of all that he is. In other words, in the case of Parama-Śiva pure consciousness means his consciousness of himself. We can understand the problem in another way. Can we say that consciousness is a capacity which we come to know only when it manifests itself, just as we come to know or become aware of our possibilities as and when they manifest themselves?

If we admit that self-consciousness of Parama-Śiva is in relation to himself and his possibilities, which he is eternally aware of, then we have to admit that the world process begins only when he desires or wishes to manifest himself or his possibilities. However, as the creative power (*spanda*) to manifest himself or his possibilities is natural to himself or is intrinsic to his nature the process of manifestation must have no beginning and end. It must be co-eternal with Parama-Śiva. Though this follows logically from the position of Kashmir Śaivism it is not acceptable to it as in that case bondage of souls, in whatever manner the nature of bondage is conceived, has to be accepted as natural, and cannot therefore be destroyed. It defeats the very purpose of Kashmir Śaivism as a religion.

To overcome this problem it is said that Parama-Śiva has a will which is autonomous, and accordingly he chooses to manifest himself as well as to withdraw the process of manifestation. This may be religiously or theologically significant and satisfying, but is not philosophically adequate and valid. It defeats the very purpose for which the solution is offered. Even if we accept that Parama-Śiva has a will which is autonomous so that he can manifest himself at will we have to explain that moment when he wills to manifest himself. If that moment can have an explanation then the autonomy of Prama-Śiva may not be an explanation. In his autonomy or freedom Parama-Śiva may as well choose not to manifest himself at all, or to manifest himself eternally. We cannot deny these possibilities which, in terms of his freedom, are as meaningful as the one preferred by Kashmir Śaivism. But if we want to opt for one choice we have to explain why the other two are not significant alternatives before Parama-Śiva. He could have chosen any or none as there is no valid reason why he should opt for one instead of the other. It is the Kashmir Śaivism that prefers one to the exclusion of others as it suits or serves its religious or theological purpose. On the other hand, if we admit that the process of manifestation has no beginning then we cannot assert, in the first place, that the world is something different from Parama-Śiva for it is the expression or manifestation of his nature. However, manifestation to be meaningful involves a process having a beginning. Otherwise we cannot use the category of possibility or potentiality. For example, we cannot say meaningfully that the sun starts manifesting itself as light because we cannot think of the sun devoid of light, or without the capacity to shine. As far as empirical experience is concerned sun's light is a matter of linguistic usage or expression as in reality there are no two things called the sun and its light. We cannot think of the sun without light, or the sun shining occasionally so that we can say that shining is not its nature. Similarly, we have to admit that the world is co-eternal with Parama-Śiva as in reality it is not something other than and different from himself. It is his nature, and Parama-Śiva cannot be without his nature. It is only when we can separate Parama-Śiva from his nature — and in that case it would not be possible to know what Parama-Śiva is — we can talk of manifestation of Parama-Śiva or his nature.

These problems cannot be avoided as long as we try to adapt Vedānta ontology to serve sectarian theological needs, either of Śaivism or Vaiṣṇavism. It is only when we think of the absolute or Parama-Śiva in terms of categories that are appropriate and meaningful to understand a human person we can speak of the absolute in such terms as *spanda-śakti* or "I-consciousness." Furthermore, to apply these categories to Parama-Śiva, and then deny them their empirical connotation when used in relation to Parama-Śiva is as good as saying nothing significant about him. To assert that Parama-Śiva is eternally self-conscious, or he is an eternal experient, and then deny the possibility of an object to it or to say that the capacity to manifest or the power of *spanda* is natural to Parama-Śiva, and yet to say that he manifests himself at will is to deny the terms their legitimate meaning. These terms when applied to a human person are highly significant and meaningful, but when they are attributed to the absolute they either prove themselves inappropriate, or show that the absolute does not really transcend empirical experience.

However, these problems cannot be avoided if one wants to adapt Vedānta or its ontology to serve the demands of a sectarian theology. God of theology cannot be identified with the *Brahman* of Vedānta without distorting the meaning of both. God of theology is not meant to solve the problems of philosophy, and the concept of *Brahman* the needs or demands of religion or theology. However, when one is sought to be integrated with the other or when God of theology is sought to be integrated with the absolute of philosophy neither philosophy nor theology is benefited. But the attempts on the part of theologians to adapt Vedānta to their respective theological positions or to reconcile *Brahman* of the Upaniṣads with the God of sectarian theologies and integrate them into a single concept, though laudable, lead to all sorts of problems. Kashmir Śaivism is one such attempt which we come across in the philosophical development of Vedānta.

6

Rāmānuja

RĀMĀNUJA is foremost among those who have tried to adapt Vedānta to suit or serve the sectarian theological needs. He is supreme among the Vaiṣṇava theologians, and a strong critic of advaita interpretation of Vedānta. Although he has not commented upon the Upaniṣads, as Śaṅkara did, he has a definite view or understanding of the meaning of the Upaniṣads as is evident from his commentary on the *Brahma-Sūtras*. He is the first to take the support of Smṛti literature, especially related to Vaiṣṇavism, in interpreting Vedānta. The *Bhāgavata Purāṇa*, a major Purāṇic text, which is more catholic and universal in its approach and outlook, and is regarded by the Vaiṣṇavas as a sacred text, was not however referred to by him in his commentary on the *Brahma-Sūtras*. It is not sectarian when compared to Vaiṣṇava or Śaiva Purāṇas, like *Viṣṇu Purāṇa* and *Śiva Purāṇa*. But Rāmānuja quotes freely from the *Viṣṇu Purāṇa* which is a major text of Vaiṣṇavism.[1] *Viṣṇu*

---

1. Generally speaking, or with the exception of *Bhāgavata Purāṇa*, the Purāṇas are sectarian in character. Their main concern is to justify and support the theological doctrines and beliefs of different sectarian religious traditions of Hinduism. Besides being an important religious text of Vaiṣṇavism, *Viṣṇu Purāṇa* is sectarian in an important sense as it denounces the Buddha and his mission in a most uncharitable manner.

   It says that the purpose of the incarnation of the Buddha is to delude (common) people against the religion of the Veda. It says: "the delusions of the false teacher paused not with the conversion of *daityas* to the Jaina and Bauddha heresies, but with

→

Purāṇa is a sectarian text as is evident from the manner in which it attacks the Buddha, and his teaching and mission. Rāmānuja refers to it extensively in support of his understanding of the nature of *Brahman*, and the way it is related to the world of empirical experience.

One may as a religious person have faith in certain things, but as a philosopher or as an interpreter of the Upaniṣads which are not sectarian, and are not even religious or theological in the ordinary sense, one is expected to be critical and non-partisan. Even when one wants to interpret the Upaniṣadic texts according to one's religious conviction and faith one has to be reasonable in his understanding and explanation as otherwise the whole exercise would be futile and insignificant. The arguments or proofs and explanations which are really meant to justify one's faith may not prove themselves helpful in understanding things objectively. A partisan or a sectarian approach and interpretation of non-sectarian texts, like the Upaniṣads, is aimed at deriving their authority and sanctity for supporting or justifying a sectarian theology. As the Upaniṣads also constitute Śruti tradition, and enjoy supreme authority as far as Hinduism is concerned every sectarian thinker or theologian has tried to derive the authority and sanctity of the Upaniṣads for their respective theological views and doctrines. They have tried to achieve two things mainly by adapting the Vedānta to their sectarian theologies. Firstly, to reconcile the Smṛti tradition with that of Śruti, and secondly to reconcile different sectarian theologies with the

---

→ various erroneous tenets he prevailed upon others to apostatize until they were led astray and deserted the doctrines and observances inculcated by the three Vedas." It says further that the Buddha preaches against the religion of the Veda by saying that the "words of authority, mighty *asuras*, do not fall from heaven. The text that has reason is alone to be acknowledged." "By such and similar lessons the *daityas* were perverted so that no one of them admitted the authority of the Vedas. They have become naked as they have thrown out the garment of the Vedas." *Viṣṇu Purāṇa* 3.18.31-35.

Vedāntic ontology or its world-view. The process of reconciliation between the traditions of Śruti and Smṛti was initiated by Vyāsa, the author of the *Mahābhārata* and the *Bhāgavata Purāṇa*. He made a very significant and comprehensive attempt to reconcile the idea of God, central to Smṛti tradition, with that of *Brahman* of Vedānta mostly at the theological or popular level. At the theological level he tried to identify *Brahman* with God, or tried to interpret *Brahman* theistically. In addition to showing or proving the personal aspect or character of *Brahman* he emphasized on the transcendental aspect of God. In emphasizing the transcendental aspect of God he wanted different sectarian religions to transcend their sectarian theologies. Thus, according to Vyāsa, God whether identified as Śiva or Viṣṇu or Śakti has a transcendental dimension, and at that level the sectarian deities lose their theological and sectarian identities, and become non-different from *Brahman* of Vedānta. Furthermore, in identifying the various sectarian deities with *Brahman*, he tried to make *Brahman* religiously more significant, as well as to make the concept of *Brahman* more meaningful to popular understanding, or to bring Vedānta to the level of people. At the same time, in identifying the various sectarian deities with *Brahman* he tried to do away with the sectarian character of the deities, and give them an identity which is more universal and impersonal. However, he tried to reconcile the traditions of Śruti and Smṛti more at the theological or popular level. The same task is sought to be achieved at a philosophical or conceptual level by theologically oriented interpreters of Vedānta, among whom Rāmānuja is foremost.

Now, it is one thing to identify the sectarian deities, like Śiva and Viṣṇu, with the Upaniṣadic *Brahman* either by way of re-defining them or by emphasizing their transcendental character, and quite another to identify *Brahman* with a sectarian deity, and attribute to *Brahman* some of the essential theological attributes or characteristics. In a sense it amounts to re-defining or re-interpreting the Upaniṣadic *Brahman* in theological terms, as well as to provide philosophical significance to what is religiously or devotionally meaningful. Such attempts may satisfy the theological needs of a sectarian religious tradition, but thereby the absolute character of *Brahman* is compromised.

In his attempt to reconcile the two kinds of Upaniṣadic statements Rāmānuja is influenced or inspired by the religious literature of Vaiṣṇavism, and tried to adapt Vedānta to Vaiṣṇava theology or to integrate Vaiṣṇava theology with Vedānta. And in the process he enriched Vaiṣṇavism, and made it more universal, and by adapting Vedānta to Vaiṣṇava theology he succeeded in providing a strong philosophical or rather ontological basis to Vaiṣṇavism. Although his attempts at reconciliation are highly significant from the point of view of Vaiṣṇavism, philosophically speaking no significant development has been achieved in understanding the problem of reconciliation between the two kinds of Upaniṣadic statements. Although Rāmānuja proved himself to be a strong critic of Advaita Vedānta, particularly its doctrine of *māyā*, as far as his own metaphysical position is concerned he was carried away by his religious faith.

Rāmānuja's identification of *Brahman* with the personal God known and worshipped in Vaiṣṇavism as Nārāyaṇa, Puruṣottama and Vāsudeva, and his dependence for authority on *Viṣṇu Purāṇa*, a Vaiṣṇava text, show that his primary concern in commenting upon the *Brahma-Sūtras* is to adapt Vedānta to Vaiṣṇavism, or more specifically Vedāntic ontology to Vaiṣṇava theology. By identifying *Brahman* of Vedānta with God as conceived in Vaiṣṇava theology and literature, and by employing Vaiṣṇava religious categories and concepts in interpreting Vedānta, especially the relationship between *Brahman* and the world, and *Brahman* and man, he tried to make Vaiṣṇavism and its theology more and more universal as well as to make it closer and acceptable to Śruti tradition. His interest in reconciling the two kinds of Upaniṣadic statements is secondary when compared to his concern for providing Vaiṣṇavism a strong philosophical basis as well as the authority of Śruti.

According to Rāmānuja's understanding of the Upaniṣads, on whom he did not comment directly, the problem of reconciliation between the two kinds of statements does not arise at all as all the Upaniṣadic statements are equally true and authoritative. Therefore, there cannot be and in reality there is no conflict or opposition between the two kinds of Upaniṣadic statements as pointed out by the earlier interpreters of Vedānta, especially Bādarāyaṇa and Śaṅkara. When all the Upaniṣadic texts and statements enjoy equal status, authority and validity trying to reconcile one kind of statements with the other kind of statements is superfluous or even meaningless. It involves seeing a conflict or opposition among the Upaniṣadic statements which in reality does not exist. When all the Upaniṣadic texts and statements are equally true and authoritative we cannot say that some of the Upaniṣadic statements are meaningful and valid only in a secondary or figurative sense. He also does not believe in the fact that some or even most of the Upaniṣadic statements have only instructional or pedagogic value and significance. However, the *Bṛhadāraṇyaka* and *Chāndogya* Upaniṣads contain large portions of Brāhmaṇa texts which have no philosophical significance. Furthermore, as the Upaniṣads are intended primarily to teach or instruct the nature and meaning of *ātman*, or *Brahman* as it reveals itself at the human level (*ādhyātmika*) they invariably take into consideration the requirements of instruction, like the level of maturity of the instructed or taught before the truth is imparted. This is evident from the various examples and analogies employed in the Upaniṣads for the purpose of instruction. The instruction imparted to Indra and Virocana about self clearly point out to the same fact. Many Upaniṣads consist of dialogues in which different views on any given problem are discussed, and at times without reaching any definite conclusion. Therefore, all the opinions or views expressed and discussed in the Upaniṣads need not necessarily represent the teaching of the Upaniṣads. This problem was discussed comprehensively in the first chapter.

Another important point to be noted in this context is the way the Upaniṣadic texts are related to the truth they represent, or the relation between truth as seen or directly and immediately experienced and the manner in which it is articulated and expressed in the Upaniṣads, or in broad terms the relation between the world-view of the Upaniṣads and the individual texts and statements of the Upaniṣads which express it. The Upaniṣadic statements do not have the same kind of meaning and validity as a statement representing an empirical fact can have. More importantly, the Upaniṣadic statements cannot be literally true as in that case there will be no need for any kind of interpretation. If what they represent is as objectively true as what an empirical statement represents the validity of the Upaniṣads can be determined in terms of what they represent. In that case there will be no need for a philosophical understanding of the Upaniṣads, and the various arguments to justify such an understanding or interpretation. And more importantly there will then be no need to integrate the meaning of various statements, and to reconcile mutually conflicting statements to get at the meaning of the Upaniṣads. In other words, we need not have to correlate and organize the Upaniṣadic statements to understand their meaning, or to develop the philosophy of the Upaniṣads. Each Upaniṣadic text or statement can then reveal the truth it represents independently of other texts and statements. Obviously all this would not be acceptable to Rāmānuja or to any interpreter of Vedānta. Rāmānuja also believes in the vision or philosophy of the Upaniṣads which is commonly reflected in all the Upaniṣadic texts and statements. On the other hand, if the need or necessity to interpret the Upaniṣads is recognized so as to find out the meaning of the Upaniṣads then certain philosophical problems cannot be avoided. The Upaniṣadic statements may not be able to reveal or express the vision or meaning of the Upaniṣads individually, but nevertheless they are the means of revealing the vision. In other words, instead of trying to understand the meaning or truth of each statement individually the Upaniṣadic statements should be understood and interpreted in relation to each other so that the vision or meaning of the Upaniṣads is comprehended.

Every interpreter, according to his understanding of the meaning of the Upaniṣads, regards some of the Upaniṣadic statements, which justify and confirm his understanding of the Upaniṣads, as central to the Upaniṣads. In this process what an interpreter omits will be more revealing that what he selects. If such of the Upaniṣadic statements in which certain ideas or doctrines concerning the nature of *Brahman* and its relationship to the world of empirical experience, including the reality of man, are taken as representing the truth of the Upaniṣads then we have to deny not only transcendental dimension to *Brahman* but also its absolute character. If *Brahman* has a transcendental dimension what is said in the Upaniṣads about *Brahman* and its nature should not be taken as definite statements. If the nature and meaning of *Brahman* can be shown in a deterministic manner the transcendence of *Brahman* will have no meaning. It also goes against the spirit or world-view of the Upaniṣads. And if we admit that *Brahman* is both immanent and transcendent then we have to accept that no statement of Śruti can determine the nature of *Brahman*, and therefore the language used in relation to *Brahman* in the Upaniṣads need not be true literally. This even the Śruti (Upaniṣads) admits when it says that its validity is until the truth is directly realized, or Śruti ceases to be valid when the truth is directly realized.[2] In other words, the Upaniṣads can only help or guide one in realizing the truth directly for himself, instead of demonstrating it as if *Brahman* is an object of demonstration. They are of instructional or means (*upāya*) value in relation to *Brahman* and its nature. They can only indicate or point to truth but not describe it. Therefore, any effort to determine and demonstrate the truth of the Upaniṣads is contrary to the spirit and vision of the Upaniṣads. A definite statement about *Brahman* may serve religious or practical purpose, but not of philosophy.

---

2. *Bṛhadāraṇyaka Upaniṣad* 4.3.22.

Another important thing we observe in the works of Rāmānuja is the lack of consistency in his understanding and criticism of Advaita. He was the first known critic or even the opponent of Advaita. He begins his exposition of Vedānta or his commentary on *Brahma-Sūtras* with the criticism of Advaita. The intention is clear. As long as the Advaita interpretation of Vedānta remains meaningful and valid his theological approach to and understanding of Vedānta may not be meaningful and valid. He, therefore, gives more importance to the criticism of rival schools, especially Advaita, before he presents his own philosophy. His seven-fold criticism of Advaita is based mainly on his analysis of consciousness and its nature. And his analysis and understanding of the nature of consciousness is based mainly on the nature of consciousness as it reveals itself in and through the states of man's empirical experience as if it is all about consciousness. It is an analysis of consciousness as it is known at the level of empirical experience or in and through the states of empirical experience. And as far as his analysis and understanding of consciousness at the level of empirical experience is concerned it is adequate and meaningful. But do the Upaniṣads and Śaṅkara speak of consciousness as it is known or revealed at the level of empirical experience in defining *Brahman* as consciousness? If consciousness means the consciousness which reveals itself at the level of empirical experience or in and through the states of empirical experience then Vedānta as expressed in the Upaniṣads, and interpreted by different Vedāntins will be utterly unintelligible. The Upaniṣads are concerned with the nature of consciousness, but in its transcendental aspect or dimension. Their main concern in analysing and understanding the nature of consciousness is to show its non-relational character which an analysis of consciousness at the empirical level cannot reveal. And without accepting the transcendental character of consciousness, which is not revealed at the level of empirical experience, our understanding of the nature of consciousness will not be complete. In itself or in its true nature consciousness is non-relational though it reveals itself at the empirical level in relation to a subject and an object. Consciousness transcends empirical experience in the sense that it is beyond the duality of subject and object which characterizes empirical experience. Though the consciousness which is revealed at the level of empirical experience is not different from the consciousness which the Upaniṣads speak about yet there is difference between our understanding of its nature and that of the Upaniṣads. Similarly, the difference between what Rāmānuja says about consciousness and what is said by Śaṅkara is meaningful in terms of its transcendental character. If consciousness has no transcendental aspect or dimension then what Rāmānuja says about it is perfectly meaningful, and true. More importantly, to deny transcendental dimension to consciousness is to deny the possibility of transcendence. And consequently we have to deny to *Brahman* what is not known through empirical experience, or what is not intelligible to our rational or empirical understanding. Then we cannot also say that *ātman* is something more than and beyond the empirical or individual self.

Now, to speak of *Brahman* as transcending consciousness and yet being within it is as unintelligible as the talk of pure consciousness. If pure consciousness is a myth, according to Rāmānuja, as it is unintelligible in terms of empirical experience and understanding, so is his understanding of *Brahman* as inhabiting consciousness and governing it. Rāmānuja tries to deny meaningfulness and validity to pure consciousness on the basis of his empirical analysis and understanding of consciousness. In that case it would not be possible to prove the validity of Vedānta, and its conception of *Brahman* in terms of empirical experience, or on the basis of empirical analysis of consciousness. Vedānta and its conception of *Brahman* are not intelligible and valid in terms of empirical experience. Similarly, to talk of *Brahman* as the self of the individual self, which is the self of the body, is empirically as unintelligible as the talk of pure consciousness. Let us take the case of body-soul relationship as formulated by Rāmānuja. It is an empirical fact that consciousness is not known independently of a living body. Consciousness means consciousness of some living being or of someone. Can we then say that both are related in the manner of a substance and its essential or primary qualities? Or is it a relationship in which we cannot think of one without the other? They cannot be separated though they can be distinguished. Let us compare this position with that of Cārvāka, according to which they are not different as one cannot exist without the other, that is a body without a soul and a soul without a body. If, according to Rāmānuja also, the body and soul are not separable as they cannot exist without each other we cannot say with sufficient justification that body only depends on the soul, but not the soul on the body for existence. The dependence will then be mutual. When both body and soul depend upon each other for their existence it is not possible to determine which of them is dependent upon the other, or which controls or governs the other. And in the absence of a body or when the body is destroyed the soul also gets destroyed as one cannot exist without the other. We are not here talking about soulless body, like a dead body, but of the existence and status of soul in the absence of a body. When the body is destroyed the soul also ceases to exist because it cannot live without a body. But the followers of Rāmānuja might say that a subtle body survives the destruction of gross body, and can form the body of the soul after the destruction of the gross body. But this is meaningful neither in terms of empirical analysis and understanding nor on the basis of rational understanding. And if it is maintained that the soul can survive the destruction of body then what happens to the relationship between body and soul which, according to Rāmānuja, is inseparability. There is no scriptural (Śruti) evidence to support the idea of subtle body. It belongs to Smṛti tradition, and is invented mainly to justify the doctrine of reincarnation. Even otherwise, on the basis of the doctrine of inseparability of body and soul we cannot think of matter as such or pure matter or matter that is not inhabited by a soul, for there can be no soul without body and a body without a soul. This is quite significant as body ordinarily or in common parlance means that which is inhabited and is used by someone. But how to understand the meaning of matter which is not a body in the above sense? We may be justified in saying that all living beings are embodied or possess bodies which are animated by a spirit or soul living within them. But what about matter or material or physical things like rocks, mountains, earth, etc. which are not living in the sense living or human beings are? Can we say that they are also inhabited by souls as living beings are? Even if we admit on the authority of scripture that they are also bodies and are therefore having souls we have to explain the sense of "soul" in their case as it cannot be the soul as we understand it in the context of living beings. Furthermore, the way the body is related to soul in the case of human beings cannot be the same in the case of other living beings. Even if we prefer to use the term soul in relation to all the living beings it cannot have the same meaning in all the cases. And when it comes to physical or material objects we cannot think of them as having souls, or think of them as bodies in the sense we define a human body or the body of a living being. We may say that in the case of a human being the body is inhabited by a soul which is distinct from the body, and whose purpose the body serves. The *Bṛhadāraṇyaka Upaniṣad* speaks of *ātman* living in all, including physical phenomena.[3] Here *ātman* is used to mean the essence or essential reality of all. It is the essence of fire, water, earth, etc. as without it they are not what they are. Nothing in the world can be what it is without its essence. Fire is known as fire or is defined as fire because of its essence, which is different from that of water. The essence of various physical phenomena is not the same as that of living beings, but, according to the Upaniṣads, it is the same *ātman* that is within all as their essence. It sustains and governs them. The same *ātman* which lives in man is known as his self or soul, or manifests itself as self. Therefore, we cannot identify the *ātman* of the Upaniṣads with the self or soul of man. A soul that lives

---

3. *Ibid.*, 7.7.3-14.

in a human body has its individual identity. It is not the same in all human beings, whereas *ātman* in the Upaniṣadic sense is a universal principle, and is present within all. *Ātman* which is the essence of all and lives within all, including physical nature, is not however related to all in the same manner. The manner in which it is related to physical nature is not the same as it is related to a human body. In a human being *ātman* is related to body as soul or self, and that is not the relationship between *ātman* and the world. Though *ātman* sustains the world by being within it as its essence it is not conscious of itself as it is in the case of human beings.

Now, if we accept Rāmānuja's interpretation of Vedānta it should follow that the physical nature or the material world is devoid of *ātman,* as the soul in the sense in which it is known in relation to man or even in relation to living beings is not present in physical nature. We do not observe physical nature being enlivened and controlled by a conscious principle called soul. This is precisely the argument Rāmānuja offers when he rejects the idea that *Brahman* manifests itself in the form of the world of empirical experience. In reply to a *pūrva-pakṣa* which maintains that the world is a manifested form of *Brahman,* Rāmānuja says:

> "consciousness must exist in the world also if it is an effect of *Brahman*" to which the *pūrva-pakṣa* replies that *Brahman* may be present in matter though it is not observed, just as consciousness though is present in man is not observed in the states of swoon and deep sleep. To this Rāmānuja replies that "permanent non-perception of intelligence in material objects proves its non-existence. This goes against what is universally observed. How can we say that a thing possesses a power of producing an effect while yet the effect is never and nowhere seen to be perceived. It is like talking to the sons of a barren woman."[4]

According to Rāmānuja, cause means the existence of something in its subtle or potential condition or state, and by effect

4. *Śrī Bhāṣya* 11.1.4.

a gross state of existence. Therefore, cause and effect are intrinsically related as what is not there in the cause cannot be found in the effect, and therefore what is in the cause must also be found in the effect, as cause and effect are not substantially different. "An effect is not a substance different from its cause but the cause itself which has passed into a different state (effect)."[5] According to such an understanding of causation, *Brahman* and world are not different substantially, and therefore the world cannot be said to be devoid of what is essential to the nature of *Brahman*. We can try to understand Rāmānuja's position in a different way. By soul-body relationship that exists either between matter and soul or soul and *ātman* we have to understand the relationship of dependence or subservience. As a human body depends on soul and subserves it so also the human soul depends upon and subserves *ātman* which is the self of *Brahman*. In other words, everything in the world, including man, depends upon *Brahman* and sub-serves him as otherwise the world will be as good as a dead body or body without a soul. It is religiously significant and satisfying to believe in the absolute supremacy of God, and the dependence of everything on him. The sense of total dependence is a highest religious virtue, according to Vaiṣṇavism. But it is one thing to accept something on faith, and quite another to develop a metaphysics or philosophy based on what one accepts on faith.

A belief or a doctrine may be religiously meaningful and satisfying, but that does not mean that it is also philosophically adequate and valid. While the meaningfulness and validity of what is religiously satisfying is limited to those who have faith in it, the validity of what is philosophically meaningful cuts across religions and religious sects. A sectarian theology is meaningful and valid to those who believe in it. But in an attempt to make it more universal some theologians try to provide a rational basis and justification to it. Such attempts though laudable end up in creating something which is neither

5 *Ibid.*, 1.4.23.

philosophy nor theology as it does not have the virtues of either. Rāmānuja who resorts to empirical analysis and logical reasoning in criticizing the views of his rivals, especially of Advaita Vedānta, abandons both while developing and upholding his own form of Vedānta. Viśiṣṭādvaita, which he has developed by way of interpreting the *Brahma-Sūtras*, is based neither on the Vedānta texts nor on rational understanding. And no Viśiṣṭādvaitin has tried to interpret the Upaniṣads, the chief and primary source of Vedānta. *Brahma-Sūtras*, which strictly speaking enjoys derived authority, and is a secondary source on Vedānta does not have the sanctity and authority of Śruti. Bādarāyaṇa is only an interpreter of Vedānta. Every interpreter of Vedānta has his own rational justification for his interpretation, and such justifications are not as sacred and authoritative as the texts of Śruti. The rational justification can be criticized and even rejected if it is not logically valid. This should be the attitude towards all interpretations of Vedānta texts, and the *Brahma-Sūtras* is not a text of Vedānta as the Upaniṣads are. And no interpretation can take the place of the text. Nevertheless, *Brahma-Ṣūtras* is a very valuable work for understanding Vedānta as it offers valuable insights into the meaning of the Upaniṣadic texts.

Let us try to understand Rāmānuja's approach to the problem of reconciliation between the two kinds of Upaniṣadic statements. How does he understand the nature of relationship between *Brahman* and the world of empirical experience? According to him, *Brahman* and the world are not identical, and at the same time they are not two and different. They are one, and at the same time different. They are related, according to Rāmānuja, in the manner of a substance and its essential qualities or a substance and its mode. However, we should not extend the significance of these examples to understand the existence of the world, but only to understand the nature of relationship between *Brahman* and the world. Rāmānuja is against applying the law of causation to *Brahman* as, according to him, *Brahman* is not the cause of the world. Nevertheless, the world has come into existence because of *Brahman* as the world is a gross form of manifestation of what is subtly present in *Brahman*. Before it manifests itself in gross form, that is in its subtle form, the world forms the body of *Brahman*. And the world comes into existence when what is subtly present in *Brahman* manifests itself into a gross form. The world is an evolution of what is potentially present in *Brahman*. While the potential state of *Brahman* is the cause, the evolved state of *Brahman* or the world is the effect, if we like to use the category of cause in understanding the world. Whatever may be the mode of its existence, the world is not substantially different from *Brahman*. But, how to understand and explain the reality of the physical or material world in terms of Rāmānuja's conception of *Brahman*? It is pure matter as we do not observe in it the existence or presence of a non-material principle or soul. This is based on repeated and universal experience. And there is the world of living beings in which we see the presence of life in the bodies of living beings. It is only in the human world we observe a soul or self living in the human body. Thus, we have a purely material or physical world, a world of living beings and a human world. How can we explain, according to Rāmānuja, the reality of all these realms which we call the world in terms of *Brahman* whose body it is. The world is the body of *Brahman*, and in him it is united or finds its oneness. According to Rāmānuja, *Brahman* is one or a unity despite the fact that he has a body. In other words, *Brahman* is one without a second despite the internal difference of body and self, and his oneness is ontological but not something that is to be achieved.

If the world is a gross form of manifestation of *Brahman* how can we find in it something that is devoid of *Brahman*'s nature, or in which *Brahman*'s essential nature is absent? Can we say that *Brahman* manifests himself partially or in parts, but not wholly? There is no pure matter in *Brahman* as his body consists of matter animated and governed by souls which in turn are governed by his self. *Brahman* is neither pure matter nor pure spirit, but an indivisible unity of both. He is one, and therefore the world as his manifestation should be an integrated whole or an indivisible unity or oneness of matter and spirit. Therefore, there can be no matter in the world which is not inhabited by a soul, as there can be no soul without a body. But the world as experienced repeatedly by all has matter which is devoid of soul. Matter that constitutes the physical world which is experienced repeatedly and universally does not show any sign of consciousness and therefore we cannot say that it is inhabited by a soul. If there were to be a soul within the matter it would have manifested itself in some form or other, but that is not, however, the case. Even if a soul in the sense we know it in relation to man is absent in matter it cannot be devoid of self of *Brahman,* as *Brahman* is the self of all that is there, including matter. Thus, if pure matter or matter devoid of soul is real as it is vouched by all the means of knowledge it cannot have *Brahman* as its source, or *Brahman*, as conceived by Rāmānuja, cannot be its explanation. *Brahman* can be an explanation of human world only. But even in the case of man also it is unintelligible to think of a self that resides in his soul which inhabits his body. It is adequate to understand human reality in terms of a body and a soul. But how to understand the reality of man in terms of a self that lives within his soul?

Now, it may be said that a soul in so far as it belongs to a person acquires its own individuality, and in terms of its individuality it is different from other souls. Is there then anything that is common to all the souls? According to Rāmānuja, what is commonly present within all the souls is the self of *Brahman*. It is commonly present within all the souls. But a soul is also a conscious principle or has knowledge as its characteristic. But Rāmānuja thinks, on the authority of *Taittirīya Upaniṣad,* that while understanding or knowledge (*vijñāna*) is the essence or characteristic of soul, bliss or *ānanda* is the essence or characteristic of self and *ānanda* is higher than *vijñāna,* the characteristic of soul.[6] As the Upaniṣad rates *ānanda* as higher than *vijñāna* there is a self in man which is higher

6 *Taittirīya Upaniṣad* 3.3.6.

than his soul. But the same Upaniṣad also speaks of *annam* or matter as *Brahman*. More significantly, in the same Upaniṣad *cit* and *ānanda* are not graded as they equally constitute *Brahman*. Therefore, it is difficult to understand why on the basis of the same Upaniṣad *ānanda* is regarded as higher than or superior to consciousness. If both constitute *Brahman* we cannot grade them and say that consciousness which forms the nature of an individual soul is lower than or inferior to bliss or *ānanda* which forms the self of *Brahman*. However, the real significance of the statements of the *Taittirīya Upaniṣad* lies in their instructional value. They are meant to teach the nature of *Brahman*, but not to identify *Brahman* with this or that. The object of the Upaniṣads is to make one understand the nature of *ātman* or *Brahman*, and in the process of instruction or teaching *Brahman* is tentatively identified with several things. The intention of the Upaniṣad is therefore not to say that *Brahman* is anyone of those things with which it is identified for the purpose of instruction. In the *Taittirīya Upaniṣad ātman* is seen as or is identified with food or body (*anna*), with vital force (*prāṇa*), with mind, with intelligence and with *ānanda*. All this is meaningful, and must have been intended by the Upaniṣad as a means or method to teach the nature of *ātman* by a process of depth analysis. It is not, therefore, valid to think that the vital self lives within the bodily self, and mental self within the vital self and so on. In the process of teaching, the teacher starts with what is gross or obvious, and guides the student to what is subtle and universal. Thus, it may not be true to the spirit of the Upaniṣads to say that the self, that is *ānanda*, lives within the soul that is intelligence or knowledge or consciousness, and the soul that is intelligence lives in the soul that is mind, and the soul that is mind lives within the soul that is body. On the other hand, these are the significant stages in the discovery of self, which when realized does not exclude anything. This is also the significance of the story of Indra and Virocana.[7]

---

7. *Chāndogya Upaniṣad* 8.7.2-4; see also 8.8.1-4.

Philosophically speaking to identify *Brahman* with God of Vaiṣṇava theology or to define *Brahman* in terms of attributes which are meaningful in relation to God may be religiously satisfying and fulfilling. But when we analyse and understand his ideas and doctrines critically or philosophically we find no logical coherence in his understanding of the problem of reconciliation of the two kinds of Upaniṣadic statements as well as the problem of the relationship between *Brahman* and the world of empirical experience. He has expressed his views on several important problems without providing any justification for them. Moreover, they are in conflict with each other, or they are not logically coherent. And no coherent system of philosophy can be developed on the basis of them. On the other hand, there would have been no philosophical problem had Rāmānuja affirmed his theological views on *Brahman* and world on the basis of faith which in reality is the case. If he really wanted to be philosophical in his approach and understanding he would have tried to transcend his personal faith in understanding the Upaniṣads. He rather tried to adapt the Upaniṣadic ontology to serve the sectarian theological needs of Vaiṣṇavism. It is, therefore, difficult to accept that his approach to and understanding of Vedānta is philosophical. He did not show the same logical rigour and acumen in understanding his own ideas and doctrines as he did in understanding and criticizing the views of others. The critical spirit he showed towards understanding Advaita should have been adopted by him in understanding his own position as well. We do not find in his writings any attempt to invent a *pūrva-pakṣa* in relation to his own views and doctrines, or before he tried to establish his own position or his interpretation of Vedānta.

7

Sri Aurobindo

AMONG the modern or contemporary Indian philosophers and thinkers it is Sri Aurobindo who made a significant and comprehensive attempt to grapple with the problem of reconciliation between the absolute and the phenomenal or *Brahman* and the world of empirical experience. In a sense, the major thrust of his philosophical writings is how to reconcile and integrate the phenomenal with the absolute. He is known for his integral approach and insightful understanding of the problems of Indian tradition in general, and Vedānta in particular. His integral approach to Indian philosophy and some of its basic problems helped him in understanding Veda and Vedānta in relation to each other which no other Indian thinker has attempted. He tried to interpret Vedānta in the light of most significant scientific discoveries so as to make it meaningful to modern or scientific man. In understanding the meaning of Vedānta he takes into consideration some of the most significant scientific discoveries, and adapts them in understanding and explaining the meaning of Vedānta. His evolutionary approach to Vedānta, or his attempt to adapt the scientific theory of evolution in understanding the basic problems of Vedānta helped him in making Vedānta intelligible to modern mind.

While Vivekānanda tried to understand the practical significance of Vedānta to modern man, or its meaning to everyday life of man, Sri Aurobindo tried to make Vedānta meaningful to modern or scientific understanding of man. Although the theory of evolution is as old as Sāṁkhya, in the

Indian tradition, it was not taken into consideration to understand and explain the basic problems of Vedānta. No significant attempt has been made by the traditional Vedāntins to understand the relevance and significance of Sāṁkhya theory of evolution in understanding and resolving the major problems of Vedānta, such as the problem of reconciliation between the absolute and the phenomenal. On the other hand, the Sāṁkhya philosophy was criticized and rejected by Śaṅkara who regarded Sāṁkhya as the main rival of Vedānta. Although the post-Śaṅkara Vedāntins made use of the concept of evolution (*pariṇāma*), they have not tried to understand its implications to Vedānta and its problems. Most of the Vedāntins have used the concept of evolution to mean manifestation. However, Rāmānuja tried to reconcile Vedānta with Sāṁkhya by trying to integrate *prakṛti* and *puruṣa* or matter and spirit in the person of *Brahman*. He used the concept of evolution *(pariṇāma)* to explain the emergence of the gross form of the world from the subtle form of it which constitutes the body of *Brahman*. The subtle form or state of the world which forms the body of *Brahman* evolves or manifests itself into gross form of the world. According to Rāmānuja, the cause and effect refer to the same reality though in its two different forms or states, namely subtle and gross, or unevolved and evolved. Rāmānuja tries to explain the existence of the world in terms of evolution or manifestation of what is subtly and potentially present in *Brahman*.

The crucial problem with the theory of evolution, as far as Vedānta is concerned, is how to reconcile or explain the reality of matter and spirit or consciousness in terms of one reality, be it pure spirit or pure matter. The Sāṁkhya philosophy did not see it possible to explain the origin of both matter and spirit in terms of one and the same reality because of the opposition between matter and spirit. They cannot co-exist in any sense or form as the presence of one is the denial or negation of the other. *Prakṛti* and *puruṣa* cannot belong to or inhere in the same reality, nor can they be integrated into one reality. On the other hand, if they can co-exist then anything can co-exist with any other thing. We have discussed in the previous chapter how the attempt of Rāmānuja to integrate the two in the person of God gives rise to philosophical problems which are insurmountable.

If there were to be no two irreconcilable realities of matter and spirit in the beginning evolution would not have been so much significant and fascinating as a cosmological theory. Had matter alone been there in the beginning evolution in the sense of becoming many would have been less problematic than if what was there in the beginning was spirit or consciousness. Although the scientific theory of evolution was originally meant to describe and explain a limited phenomenon of biology, the sphere of its operation or application has been soon extended by philosophers to cover or include the whole world. If evolution is a fact, though valid scientifically within a limited range of human experience, it may hold the key to understanding the whole of human experience. Many have thought that a coherent philosophical interpretation of it may prove to be significant in solving some of the riddles concerning the origin of the world, its destiny, and the place of man in it. However, reflection on the scientific theory of evolution gives rise to certain deeper problems such as, what is it that is evolving, why is it evolving and what would be the goal or destiny of the process of evolution? Though these problems are outside the scope of scientific inquiry and understanding, without an adequate understanding of them we may not be able to grasp the full significance of the theory of evolution. Thus, immediately after its discovery some philosophers have tried to find in it a significant explanation of the origin of the world. And some philosophers have developed metaphysical theories or doctrines around the concept of evolution. While the approach of philosophy is purely rational some others have followed a different approach, and tried to understand the meaning of cosmic evolution with the help of or in the light of certain religious insights. Among the religious thinkers and mystics who viewed man in an evolutionary perspective, the Sūfī poet and mystic Rūmī may be the foremost. He envisaged man not only as emerging from the lower forms of nature, but also as evolving further in spirit to higher and higher levels till the whole process of evolution is consummated in his realization of God, the oneness or unity of all.[1]

In India Sāṁkhya was a bold attempt to explain the origin and destiny of the world in terms of evolution though it was not pursued further for a long time. However, its impact or influence must have been powerful and pervasive for we find it being criticized and refuted by most of the philosophers of India. However, they have tried to incorporate or integrate its basic insights into their own thought or philosophy.

Among the modern Indian thinkers and philosophers Sri Aurobindo stands as a shining example among those who have tried to construct a coherent system of Vedānta philosophy meaningful to modern or scientific mind. He tried to understand the meaning of Vedānta in the light of the concept of evolution. He also saw in the concept of evolution a meaningful means to resolve some of the basic problems of Vedānta. It is a rare combination that men of spiritual *sādhanā* and realization try to relate and integrate their spiritual insights with those of science as scientists trying to relate their findings or discoveries with the basic spiritual or religious insights of humankind. We find in the philosophy of Sri Aurobindo, a serious and significant attempt to relate and integrate his spiritual insights with those of science.

---

1. *Rumi: Poet and Mystic: Selections from his Writings*, tr. Reynold A. Nicholson, London: George Allen and Unwin Ltd., 1956, p. 103.

   I died a mineral and became a plant,
   I died as plant and rose to animal,
   I died as animal and I was man.
   Why should I fear? When was I less by dying?
   Yet once more I shall die as Man, to soar
   With angels blest, but even from angelhood
   I must pass on; all except God doth perish.
   When I have sacrificed my angel-soul,
   I shall become what no mind ever conceived.
   Oh, let me not exist, for Non-existence
   Proclaims in organ tones. To him we shall return — Poem LXI

Although Sri Aurobindo's concern with philosophy or his integral approach to problems of philosophy is more comprehensive or wider than to defend or justify any particular religion or philosophy, yet his understanding of Vedānta or his interpretation of it in the light of the concept of evolution is a significant step or landmark in the philosophic development of Vedānta. He found in the theory of evolution a significant means or method to achieve reconciliation between the absolute and the phenomenal or *Brahman* and the world. While the scientific theory of evolution is meant to explain the process of the emergence of different forms or species of life, including man, Śrī Autobindo's concern with it is to understand and explain the "why" and "wither" of evolution. Science is concerned only with the explanation of "how" and leaves unexplained "why" and "wither" of evolution. Sri Aurobindo is not so much interested in understanding the outer form or process of evolution, but in understanding the inner process or dynamics of evolution which is reflected clearly in the evolution of human spirit or the evolution of consciousness in man. His conception of evolution is basically spiritual, and his approach to it is intuitive and religious. By spiritual evolution he means the spiritual progression of man, or the evolution of consciousness from the in-conscient or un-conscient stage through life and mind to super-conscient or supramental stage. In and through all the stages of evolution, either in nature or in man, the same being has been evolving or unfolding its own possibilities by virtue of a force or energy (*śakti*) which is inherent within itself. "This is what we call evolution which is an evolution of consciousness and evolution of the spirit in the things and outwardly an evolution of species."[2] The scientific theory of form evolution acts only as a clue or an indicator to the inner evolution of the spirit which manifests itself in and through the outer forms of evolution also. If spirit is the ultimate source and essence of evolution phenomenal evolution or evolution of forms is only an outward mani-

2. *Complete Works of Sri Aurobindo*, vol. 22, p. 44.

festation of what is taking place within that process. And unless we are able to discover the inner workings of the spirit, the real essence or meaning of evolution, the visible or the outward aspect or form of evolution may fail to convey any meaning. And a theory of evolution which does not take into consideration the essential aspect or characteristic of evolution will remain inconclusive. The real significance or meaning of evolution cannot be found out at the process level but in that of which the outward process is only an unfoldment or manifestation. It creates the outer forms out of itself to serve as its instruments of expression and fulfilment. In this sense, spiritual evolution is not the same as the scientific concept of evolution, and according to Sri Aurobindo, the former is a self-evident fact of our spiritual life having its own logic and justification.

The fundamental problem of spiritual evolution is: "what is that which is growing within us but into which we have not yet grown?"[3] It is in man the process of evolution becomes self-conscious, or takes a conscious turn. Man stands at the turning point or he is the turning point in the process of evolution which passes from the stage of unconsciousness in matter to self-consciousness in man. "Man is nature's great term of transition in which she grows conscious of her aim; in him she looks up from the animal with open eyes towards her divine ideal."[4] The brief discussion of the meaning of evolution, according to Sri Aurobindo, will help us in understanding and appreciating the purpose or intention of Sri Aurobindo in adapting the concept of evolution to Vedānta.

Besides the concept of evolution he has taken certain ideas from the Indian religious tradition, more specifically Śākta tradition, in understanding the meaning of Vedānta. According to Śākta tradition, consciousness is a dynamic principle in the sense that the power to manifest itself or its possibilities is

---

3. *Ibid.*, vol. 15, p. 219.

4. *Ibid.*, vol. 16, p. 279.

inherent within itself. Consciousness is never devoid of its power to manifest itself, and in terms of its power it becomes what it is capable of becoming, or manifests all that it is capable of becoming. In other words, consciousness, which forms the nature of *Brahman*, evolves itself so that it can realize itself fully in the sense that it can realize itself in and through all that it is capable of becoming. Thus, the world as the becoming of *Brahman* is real, and the concept of evolution helps us in understanding the manner in which *Brahman* becomes the world. Being and becoming, according to Sri Aurobindo, are the two states or modes of the absolute or *Brahman* whose nature, however, cannot be defined or determined in terms of either.

The idea of evolution presupposes, according to Sri Aurobindo, the concept of involution, and therefore what is being manifested in the process of evolution is already present in the being though in an unmanifested or unevolved state or condition. Evolution is the process whereby what is already present in the absolute becomes manifest. The absolute realizes all its possibilities in and through the process of evolution, just as a seed realizes its possibilities in becoming a tree. The tree is the realization, as it were, on the part of the seed of its possibilities, or the seed realizes itself fully when it becomes a tree. The tree is not, therefore, different from the seed as it is a manifested or evolved form of the seed. The absolute or *Brahman* comes to realize itself or its possibilities fully in and through the process of evolution, and therefore the self-realization on the part of the absolute means realizing or seeing itself in all its manifestations. And all the manifestations of the absolute reveal it though its nature cannot be determined in terms of any one of its manifested forms. However, the nature of the absolute cannot be determined in terms of its manifested forms because the possibility of its future manifestation will always be there. While in the case of an animal or a tree we can to a large extent determine the limits of their evolution we cannot do so in the case of man, and more so in the case of the absolute. In the case of man though his physical evolution has reached its limits or has come to an end his spiritual evolution is still an ongoing process, and according to Sri Aurobindo, man is abnormal in the sense that he does not yet know what is normal to him.[5] We cannot say with certainty what is it to be a normal human being as we can say about an animal or a tree.

Does this mean that the possibilities of the absolute are endless or infinite so that it is not possible to determine the end or goal of evolution? It is not possible to provide a clear solution to this problem. If we say that the spiritual evolution reaches its end or goal when man realizes the absolute in and through all that it has become we will be trying to determine the absolute and its nature, but on the other hand, if we say that the absolute is all that it has become, and at the same time it is something more than what it has become then no definition of the absolute will be adequate. And if we accept such a position we cannot think of or foresee the end or goal of evolution as the possibilities of the absolute are endless or infinite. It also negates or contradicts the concept of involution. In the case of a seed we can foresee what all it can become because the tree which is involved in the seed has finite possibilities. But as the possibilities of the absolute are infinite its realization of all its possibilities involves endless time, and therefore the idea of involution in relation to absolute is not meaningful. If the possibilities of a thing are to be involved in it they are to be realized first, and only limited or finite possibilities can be realized in time. And unless the possibilities are already involved in a thing they cannot be evolved as the ideas of involution and evolution, according to Sri Aurobindo, presuppose each other. In other words, evolution is possible because of involution, and involution is possible because of evolution. Without involution we cannot think of evolution. Any kind of change is not evolution, or evolution is not just change having no determinable purpose or goal because the process of evolution brings out or manifests what is already

5. *Life Divine*, Chapter 23; see also chapter 6.

there in a thing, or what is involved in it. This is true empirically because a seed evolves itself into what it is capable of becoming, and what it is capable of becoming is already present within itself though in a potential form of existence. But when we try to understand the emergence of the world due to evolution on the part of the absolute or *Brahman* we face logical or metaphysical problems.

As pointed out earlier, if involution is not meaningful with regard to the absolute how can we explain the process of evolution in terms of the absolute. Here it may be argued that actualization or realization of all the possibilities is not necessary to understand the concept of involution in relation to the absolute. It is sufficient to accept that the absolute has all the possibilities which can evolve into the world. We may equate potential with involution, and say that the world is an actualization of what is potentially present within the absolute. This involves the idea of *satkāryavāda*, according to which, the effect is already present in the cause as anything cannot be the cause of anything else. Unless the cause has already within itself the effect it cannot give birth to the effect, and this presupposes the idea of involution as we cannot relate two things as cause and effect if there is nothing that is common between them. But if we accept that evolution is not meaningful without involution then we have to admit our earlier position that involution is not meaningful or possible with regard to *Brahman*. And in the absence of the possibility of involution with regard to *Brahman* we cannot also talk of evolution on the part of *Brahman*. However, the popular or Smṛti form of Hinduism believes in periodic creation and destruction of the world which is meaningful only in terms of God who can create or destroy the world at will, but not when we think of creation as having no beginning as it is a manifestation of what is potentially present in the ultimate reality. As creation of the world means the gross form of its manifestation, in the state of dissolution the world returns to its subtle form of existence. However, when we try to understand and present such a religious belief philosophically all the logical problems arise, and they cannot be ignored as long as one is philosophical in his approach.

Now, let us try to understand whether spiritual evolution or evolution of spirit or consciousness is philosophically a meaningful idea. The evolution of matter, including organic matter, is intelligible, as matter evolves or undergoes change because of circumstances, and in the process of such a change or evolution varied new forms come into existence or emerge. And in turn their interaction with each other may give rise to newer forms, and thus the process of evolution may go on endlessly as the whole process of evolution of matter is unintelligent, and hence devoid of purpose. But in the case of man, a self-conscious being, growth or evolution is not only physical but also mental. Man grows both physically and mentally. Although the physical growth is the same in all, and has the same end, mental growth is not the same in all the human beings. We are not talking of consciousness here as we cannot think of growth of consciousness unless we are prepared to identify it with mind or understanding. While physical growth in man is natural, and follows the laws of nature, mental growth is not a natural process. We cannot say that the mental growth in human beings is as natural as the physical growth. While the physical growth follows the laws of evolution, mental growth is not, strictly speaking, law-governed though psychology tries to discover the laws governing the growth of human mind. The intellectual achievements of all the human beings are not the same. Even within a given culture or civilization the mental or intellectual growth of all its members is not the same. It is only a few individuals who contribute to the growth and glory of man, and they are an exception to the law, if there is one that governs the growth of human mind. The point we are trying to make is that the intellectual growth in human beings does not, strictly speaking, follow any fixed law. The creative persons, inspired people and geniuses are not, strictly speaking, governed by the law of evolution which seems to govern ordinary people. Similarly we cannot regard the Buddha or

Jesus or the seers of the Upaniṣads as less evolved for they belong to the past, or were born much before the modern man who is considered to have achieved a level of evolution. Thus though we can determine the laws that govern the physical growth of man we cannot with the same level of accuracy determine the laws that govern the growth of human mind or intelligence. Growth of human mind is a conscious process. Furthermore, it may be true to say that the spiritual growth of man does not so much depend on time as his physical growth. If human mind also obeys the law of evolution then we cannot explain certain facts of human life like intuition, inspiration, etc. More importantly, the human achievements of past should have no meaning and validity for us who are more evolved which however is not the case.

But in a sense it is meaningful to talk of evolution with regard to man and his possibilities. Man has to evolve or grow to come to know or realize his own possibilities, just as a seed has to grow into a tree to realize its possibilities. At no point of time in his growth man comes to know or realize all that he is capable of becoming, or all his possibilities. He has to grow to know all that he is capable of growing into, and growth involves process or time. Even if we accept that evolution is true of human growth, both physical and mental, still there is something in man which does not grow or evolve, and that is the fact of consciousness. Man is aware of his growth, both physical and mental, or is aware of the unfoldment of his personality, or the realization of his possibilities. But we cannot say that the awareness underlying the process of growth also undergoes change, or is itself a process. There is growth in man's understanding of himself and of the world, and therefore it may appear that there is also growth in human spirit or consciousness. However, this is relevant to understand the main problem of evolution with regard to *Brahman* or the absolute. Man has to grow or evolve to know or realize his own possibilities or what he is capable of becoming. Does *Brahman*'s knowledge of itself depend upon its becoming or evolving itself into all that it is capable of becoming? Is it meaningful to think that *Brahman* knows itself and becomes all only when it becomes all as a result of evolution? Similarly, can we say that in realizing *Brahman* one does not realize all at the same time? Does self-realization on the part of man, according to Vedānta, mean realization of his *ātman* which is not *Brahman,* and therefore not all? Is *Brahman*-realization an interpretation of self-realization in which one realizes his self only, but not his identity with *Brahman* and all? We can understand this problem with the help of an analogy of knowing gold. However, the analogy should not be extended to all aspects as gold is a physical reality. Is it not true to say that to know gold is to know it wherever and whenever it is seen in any form, but not to know any particular piece of gold or all gold? If, on the other hand, to know gold is to know all gold then one can never know what gold is as it is not possible for him to know all the gold. At the same time one cannot say that he does not know gold because he has not seen all the gold. Similarly in realizing *ātman* one does not know it as conditioned or limited by body and mind, for in realizing *ātman* one transcends all the factors that condition or limit *ātman.* And when all the factors that limit or condition *ātman* are transcended in realizing *ātman* there will be no sense in maintaining that in realizing *ātman* one realizes oneself only, but not the self that is within all. However, we may accept that self-realization is not the same as *Brahman*-realization, and therefore in realizing oneself one does not at the same time realize *Brahman* and all. But can we apply the same logic to *Brahman*? Even with regard to man, and his self-realization we face problems. Self-realization in the sense of realizing all that one is capable of becoming, or realizing all his possibilities may not be possible for two reasons. No one can be said to have realized himself till he has realized all his possibilities. But how can anyone know whether he has realized all his possibilities? Does it involve time? If we accept that self-realization involves time, and is the result of a process we cannot say whether one has realized himself and all his possibilities, or whether the process has reached its end.

What is the meaning of self-realization in the case of man? Can we say that man realizes himself when he realizes his essential being or his real nature which is common to all? To know the meaning of humanity we need not observe all the human beings past and future which is not possible, and for that reason we cannot say that we do not know the meaning of humanity. Can we say meaningfully that *Brahman*'s knowledge of itself depends upon its knowing all its possibilities or all that it is capable of becoming? Or is it the case that *Brahman* knows all in knowing itself? Can we say that though in reality *Brahman* is all, it does not know itself as all until it becomes all, and therefore has to depend upon its becoming all to know itself. In the *Bṛhadāraṇyaka Upaniṣad* it is said that supposing man becomes all by knowing *Brahman*, — "what did *Brahman* know because of which it became all."[6] In reply it is said: "In the beginning *Brahman* is all that is. It knew itself as "I am *Brahman*," and therefore it became all. And anyone who knows it (*Brahman*) becomes *Brahman*, and all."[7] On the other hand, it is only when we can think of *Brahman* which is not all, or the state of *Brahman* before it has become all, we may be justified in thinking that *Brahman* becomes all due to its knowledge of itself as all. It is meaningful to think that a seed comes to know itself as tree only when it has become the tree because to know the seed is not the same as to know the tree, or to know clay is not the same as to know a pot. But it is not meaningful to say that one knows *Brahman*, and yet does not know all as by definition *Brahman* is all. But we may maintain that one may know oneself, and yet may not know his oneness with all. Then what makes one realize his oneness with all? If we say that it is one's knowledge of *Brahman* then we have to explain as to what makes one realize that *Brahman* is all? Can we say that self-realization is different from *Brahman*-realization and *Brahman*-realization is different from the realization that *Brahman* is all? Even if we suppose

6. *Bṛhadāraṇyaka Upaniṣad* 1.4.9.

7. *Ibid.*,1.4.10.

that they are different we have to explain the way they are related, or how one comes to realize *Brahman* as all after the realization of *Brahman*? In the case of seed and tree one can know them as different. Therefore, the knowledge of one does not mean or involve the knowledge of the other. One may know the seed without knowing the tree, and vice versa.

According to Sri Aurobindo, being and becoming constitute the reality of the absolute, and therefore in realizing any one aspect of the absolute the other is not realized simultaneously. The realization of the transcendental aspect of the absolute is only a step towards realizing the other or dynamic aspect of the absolute. And unless all the aspects of the absolute are realized the absolute is not known fully. As man is an individual, and at the same time an integral part of the cosmic whole, and as both of them are the real manifestations of the absolute, to realize the absolute in its transcendental aspect is not the same as to realize it fully and integrally. To know the absolute in its transcendental aspect is not the same as to know it in its dynamic aspect as the world of manifestation. Similarly, to see *Brahman* in its manifested form or as being present in the world is not the same as to know it in its transcendental aspect. *Brahman* is to be realized in both of its aspects to have an integral (*pūrṇa*) knowledge of it. Towards such knowledge of the absolute individual salvation is only a first step. In other words, self-*Brahman*-unity realization is not the same as All-*Brahman*-realization. Realization of *Brahman* is incomplete without the realization of its oneness with all. Though both being and becoming constitute the reality of the absolute, by realizing the being of the absolute one does not automatically realize the becoming of the absolute. What is then the relationship between being and becoming, or how are they related to the absolute?

However, the fact that someone has known or realized *Brahman* shows that *Brahman* is all, as man's existence indicates the state of *Brahman*'s manifestation. Let us take the example of gold. One comes to know gold by seeing a piece of gold, and thereafter whenever he sees another piece of gold he sees gold in it. Can we say that one knows *Brahman* first, and afterwards comes to see its presence or manifestation in all? This problem gives rise to a more basic problem of what is *Brahman* before it has become all. Can we say that *Brahman* and all refer to two distinct or different realities? If we can think of *Brahman*, which is not all, then we have to admit a space in which all can come into existence. On the other hand, if *Brahman* and all refer to the same reality, and are co-extensive then in realizing one the other is realized. They are not different though conceptually they can be distinguished. In other words, to say that one has realized *Brahman* but has not realized its oneness with all, or vice versa makes no sense unless we are prepared to admit that *Brahman* is a limited or finite reality. But by definition *Brahman* is all, and the Śruti statements like "I am *Brahman*" and "all is *Brahman*" are two ways of expressing the same truth, or express the same truth from two different points of view. The object of the statements is to negate wrong knowledge that one is not *Brahman*, and the world or all is not *Brahman*. The statements do not refer to two different states of realization. The significance of the two statements can be appreciated in terms of the two contexts in which they are made. "I am *Brahman*" in reality means "I am all" or *ātman* is *Brahman* means *ātman* is all. They do not refer to two different states of realization or to two different visions. However, to understand the significance of the statements we have to remember the context in which they are made.

But the crucial problem is why we experience the world of differences in which all the categories of human understanding are perfectly meaningful and valid. There is matter, and there is consciousness, and both are real as far as the empirical experience is concerned. But what happens to the world of empirical experience when *Brahman* is realized? Can we say that the world of empirical experience ceases to be the moment *Brahman* is realized? In other words, what is the reality of the world of empirical experience? If we say that it has no reality how to explain the fact that we all experience it. We experience the world of differences, but if we accept the authority of those who have directly realized *Brahman* the world of our empirical experience is not real. That means either the world of empirical experience is real, or *Brahman* is real as both cannot be real objectively. We can understand this problem with the help of another scientific discovery. From the point of view of science what we experience as a solid material world is not really there though we experience it. What we ordinarily experience as something solid is in reality something different. However, both are real though from the points of view of two different experiences. And there is no point of transition between the two as far as the reality is concerned. The same reality is experienced in two different forms, or there are two different experiences of the same reality, one ordinary experience and the other of science. The same reality is experienced in one way by ordinary man and differently by a scientist or physicist. And we cannot say that the reality undergoes change corresponding to two different experiences of itself, for both the experiences are possible at the same time though not for the same person. However, the scientific discovery cannot be taken as the final truth. And no scientist has tried to explain as to why what appears to a scientist in one way appears differently to an ordinary person when there is no change in the nature of the reality. How to explain the difference in experience of the same reality when there is no change in the nature of reality? It is a different problem as to which experience is valid ultimately. However, the sense of mystery we face or the perplexity we experience when we try to understand the problem rationally, is what is really indicated by the term *māyā*, and is so used by the classical Advaitins, especially Śaṅkara.

In almost all the solutions to the problem of reconciliation between the absolute and the phenomenal, or *Brahman* and the world of empirical experience provided by the philosophers attempts are made to comprehend the meaning of the absolute in terms of categories derived from empirical experience, and are meaningful and valid within the realm of empirical experience. Categories of empirical understanding are employed to understand the meaning of the absolute as otherwise the absolute may not be intelligible. In other words, to make the absolute intelligible in terms of rational understanding we extend the scope of empirical categories to the absolute. Thus, we face a situation in which we either deny existence to the absolute as it is not intelligible to our empirical or rational understanding, or bring it within the purview of rational understanding. But both the options are not acceptable to many Vedāntins. If the absolute is amenable to categories of empirical understanding it becomes a part of the empirical reality. If the categories of empirical understanding are meaningful in relation to a reality, or the reality to which we can apply at least the categories of space and time then that reality cannot be *Brahman*. Therefore, we have to admit that either the world or *Brahman* is objectively real as both cannot be real at the same time, and in the same sense. And even if they can exist we cannot understand and judge their reality in terms of the categories which are appropriate and significant in relation to one or the other. Therefore, the question of finding out the relationship between them does not arise as both cannot exist, and be real in the same sense. The validity of the Upaniṣadic statements which speak about one cannot be understood and judged in terms of the statements which speak about the other. However, most of the Vedāntins in their zeal to defend or justify the reality of the empirical world, or the world of empirical experience, have tried to define *Brahman* in empirically or rationally meaningful terms, and unwittingly make it a part of empirical reality.

Sri Aurobindo tries to understand the nature of consciousness in dynamic terms so that the reality of the world of empirical experience can be firmly established. According to him, other Vedāntins, especially classical Advaitins like Saṅkara, could see only its static nature. They view consciousness as devoid of all activity and dynamism. But, according to Sri Aurobindo, the absolute is both static and dynamic, or both being and becoming. And if the absolute is to be identified with pure consciousness then the nature of consciousness is to be viewed and understood in dynamic terms. According to Sri Aurobindo, consciousness is force or power. Now, we have to turn to man to understand the nature of consciousness, and the manner of its manifestation, because man is the key to understand the nature of consciousness. Man is a self-conscious being, and in him consciousness reveals or manifests itself in and through such acts as perception, thinking, imagination, feeling, etc. or in and through all the mental acts. Therefore, in their absence it is also not known. At the same time as what is commonly revealed in and through all the mental acts consciousness is distinct from the mental acts. It cannot, therefore, be identified with any one or all the mental acts. Is it then possible for us to think of consciousness as such or independently of mental acts? Although it is logically possible to view consciousness as distinct from its manifestations, in reality it is not known without its manifestation. Then what sort of relationship can exist between consciousness and its manifestations? Obviously it is not one of being and becoming. While some have tried to reduce consciousness to the various forms of its manifestation or expression, others have tried to understand it as a substance manifesting itself in and through its various manifestations or functions. And if it is not possible to think of consciousness without its manifestations they may not be really different. However, the need to ıelate the two arises only when a difference is made between them. Now, this problem gives rise to a more important problem. As perception, thinking, etc. or any mental act is not possible without an object or an idea, which they reveal, is there any relationship, other than that of knower-known or subject-object one, between consciousness and the things it reveals. Here is the point of departure between the classical Advaita of Śaṅkara and the "realistic Advaita" of Sri Aurobindo. While, according to Sri Aurobindo, the relationship is one of being and becoming, according to

Śaṅkara, there cannot be any relationship between them as they are not two in reality. According to Śaṅkara, all that is there is *Brahman*, but in the absence of such realization *Brahman* is viewed as something different from oneself and all. Therefore, in realizing one's oneness with *Brahman* one realizes simultaneously one's oneness with all as all is not in reality different from *Brahman*. However, as one views the universe, the individual selves and *Brahman* as different from each other, the need to relate each with the other and all with *Brahman* is significant. However, when *Brahman* is directly realized the problem of relating the world with *Brahman* or *Brahman* with all disappears, as in reality *Brahman* is all that is there. On the other hand, if *Brahman* is not really all, or in realizing it all is not realized simultaneously, then *Brahman* would only be a concept, or a void, or a mere nothing.

We can view and understand the problem of reconciliation in a different way. How to reconcile ultimately the fact of universal dynamism with the unchanging character of the absolute? How to explain the process of becoming and its validity in terms of the absolute? Is it meaningful to explain becoming positively in terms of the absolute? In other words, can we take away from the notion of *māyā* its enigmatic character, and make it really intelligible to rational understanding of man? If the idea of the absolute as conceived in traditional Advaitic terms is accepted, the problem of explaining change and dynamism in realistic and positive terms gives rise to the problem of *māyā*. In trying to overcome the problem of *māyā* attempts are made to understand the nature of *Brahman* in the light of the philosophy of Tantra. According to Tantra, consciousness is force or power (*citśakti*), and therefore the process of world creation or the process of becoming is a creative play of consciousness (*cid-vilāsa*) or a spontaneous outflow of *Brahman*'s nature. Thus, if we view consciousness as a dynamic and creative power constituting the nature of the absolute or *Brahman*, the problem of explaining the world in positive terms or the problem of self-manifestation of *Brahman* will not be insurmountable. Do we then have to deny the immutable character of *Brahman*? No, says Sri Aurobindo. According to him both being and becoming or immutability and dynamism or change constitute the nature of *Brahman* which, in itself, is more than and beyond them. "Becoming which is a true movement of Being, and both Being and Becoming are truths of one absolute reality."[8] They are only the ways in which *Brahman* manifests itself. The absolute as pure possibility of all that is, and all that can be cannot really be absolute unless it has in itself the power to manifest or actualize all its possibilities. Becoming expresses Being, or Being finds itself in all its dynamic becoming. Becoming is the effectual aspect of Being. "It is a dynamic power and result, a creative energy and working out of Being, a constantly persistent yet, mutable form, process, outcome of its immutable formless essence."[9] Could this be a meaningful solution to the problem of reconciliation?

If being and becoming constitute the essential nature of *Brahman* what could be the relationship between these aspects or dimensions or modes of *Brahman*, and how both of them are integrated in the nature of *Brahman*? If dynamism is viewed as intrinsic to the nature of *Brahman* then the process of change or becoming is to be conceived as incessant or co-eternal with the absolute. On the other hand, if we think of *Brahman* in terms of its essential immutable character or as being we have to deny change of any kind in the nature of *Brahman*. But how to understand them as constituting the nature of *Brahman*, or how to understand their co-existence within the same reality? Do they not cancel each other? To avoid such a problem can we say that *Brahman* alternates its nature, that is to say, one aspect of *Brahman* manifesting itself at a time. If *Brahman* is to alternate its nature from being to becoming and then from becoming to being, and so on, what will be the logic of such alternation? Even then they cannot operate together or manifest themselves simultaneously for it is logically impossible

8. *Complete Works of Sri Aurobindo*, vol. 19, p. 637.

9. *Ibid.*, vol. 19, p. 65.

to conceive such a state. It may then be argued that we cannot in terms of our logical understanding comprehend the mystery or the logic of *Brahman*.[10] Then in what sense could this be a better explanation than the one provided by classical Advaita in terms of *māyā*, except that it tries to justify our attachment and concern for the world of empirical experience. To avoid this difficulty if we say that the absolute in itself is both being and becoming, and yet transcends them both it would be tantamount to admitting the failure of our rational understanding in coming to grips with the problem meaningfully. In an attempt to overcome such a problem if we try to give a new meaning to *Brahman* according to the demands of our logical understanding, or till we are able to explain the world process positively, then such conceptions of *Brahman* will have no validity better than that of an imaginary entity. It will also have no foundation in human experience or the authority of Śruti. On the other hand, if we come to realize the failure of reason or the limits of rational understanding in explaining the process of becoming in terms of the absolute or *Brahman* then we have to accept the meaningfulness of *māyā* which in reality stands to signify such failure.

All the categories of our understanding and conceptual frameworks can meaningfully operate only within the world of becoming or in the world of empirical experience. And if we want to say anything about that which is not within the world of empirical experience, or a part of it then the categories

---

10. Despite his brilliant attempt to develop a positive attitude to the problem of reconciliation between the absolute and the phenomenal or *Brahman* and the world, Sri Aurobindo admits that the logic and the categories that are meaningful and valid with regard to the phenomenal cannot be applied meaningfully and validly to the absolute. In this context he says the logic of the absolute is magic to ordinary understanding of man. He admits that a "certain kind of agnosticism is the final truth of all knowledge." "God is infinite possibility. Therefore, Truth is never at rest."

    Complete works, vol. 17, p. 87; *The Life Divine*, p. 14.

and concepts which are valid and meaningful within the realm of empirical experience lose their meaningfulness and validity. They lose their power to understand and explain when applied to the absolute or *Brahman*. In other words, what is meaningful and valid about things which are within a system cease to be meaningful and valid when applied to the system as such. It is meaningful and valid to say that things in the world move within space and develop within time, and are bound by the law of causation. But if we try to understand the absolute or *Brahman* or all that is there in terms of the categories of space, time and causation we will have to face an absurd situation. The movement within the world is meaningful but to think of the movement of the world or the absolute is not so. Thus, what may be meaningful and valid with regard to the phenomenal world may not be so with regard to the absolute. And if we think that the absolute has its logic, and the phenomenal world another, what will the meeting point between the two, or what will be the point of transition between the two? If the logic of one is not the same as that of the other, and if we are within the system of one logic how can we make the other system meaningful in terms of our system of logic? This leads to all types of fallacies. The problem of transition from the logic of the absolute to that of the phenomenal world, or vice versa has baffled many in the past, and will continue to baffle in future also. The way out of it is not to appeal to a higher logic of which we have no clear idea. Even the higher logic or the logic of higher minds is still human, and hence falls within the phenomenal realm only. To comprehend the nature of the absolute is to give up our logic born of the phenomenal world or the empirical experience, and move beyond it. Spiritual things are not meaningful and intelligible in terms of our empirical understanding. And unless one is given up or transcended the other is not appreciated and realized. We cannot and in reality do not live in both the worlds at the same time. The highest or the absolute when realized bestows a new meaning to the lower or the phenomenal reality, but not vice versa.

Glossary

Ādhibhautika	:	According to the Veda, all that is there is classified into three realms of *ādhibhautika, ādhidaivika* and *adhyātma*, and the divine is seen as present within all the realms. *Ādhibhautika* refers to the realm of physical reality.
Ādhyātmika	:	Manifestation and revelation of the divine at the level of human reality or within the reality of man.
Āraṇyakas	:	They form part of Vedic literature, and contain discussions and insights on some of the basic problems of philosophy.
Apauruṣeya	:	The Veda is regarded as impersonal as the truth or wisdom it contains is not due to any human agency. It has no human origin; it is divinely inspired.
Ārṣa-darśana	:	As seen or realized by a sage.
Bhagavad-Gītā	:	An integral part of *Mahābhārata*, and is regarded as one of the basic texts of Vedānta.
Brahma	:	In the Veda, it is used primarily to mean divinely inspired devotion, and by extension to prayer, the means of expression of devotion and to hymn.
Brahma-Sūtras	:	One of the basic texts of Vedānta, and consists of aphorisms. It deals mainly with the philosophical problems of Vedānta.

Brāhmaṇas	:	They form part of Vedic literature, and deal mainly with the Vedic rites and rituals.
Cārvāka	:	Represents the materialist tradition in Indian philosophy.
Hiraṇyagarbha	:	Refers to a cosmic form of manifestation of *Brahman*.
Īśvara	:	Refers to *Brahman* conceived in relation to the world and its creation.
Kapila	:	The founder of Sāṁkhya system of philosophy.
Kavi	:	In the Veda it refers to a person who is divinely inspired, and sees the divine in the varied forms of its manifestation.
Kāvya	:	The creative work of a *kavi*, and the world is seen as a *kāvya* of the divine in the Veda.
Kashmir Śaivism	:	One of the major schools of Śaivism. It is also known as Śivādvaita as Śiva is identified in it with *Brahman* of Advaita.
Māyā	:	An enigmatic category or principle meant to explain the origin and nature of the world.
Pūrṇa	:	Sri Aurobindo characterizes his Advaita as *pūrṇa* or integral as in it nothing is denied or negated.
Prajñā	:	Wisdom or consciousness, and is identi-fied with *Brahman* in the Upaniṣads.
Prajāpati	:	*Brahman* conceived in relation to living beings.
Prakṛti	:	According to Sāṁkhya, it is one of the two ultimate principles which can explain the existence of the world. It is the explanation of the world except the spirit or self.

Pūrva-Mīmāṁsā : One of the main schools of Vedic interpretation in which ritual action (*dharma*) is seen as the meaning of the Veda.

Pūrva-pakṣa : Presentation and discussion of a rival position before it is analysed and criticized.

Ṛṣi : In the Veda it refers to a divinely inspired person who sees the world of manifestation in its divine unity.

Sādhanā : Preparation required to attain or realize the end or goal in view.

Śaivism : One of the major sects of Hinduism. It regards and worships Śiva as God or the ultimate reality.

Saṁhitā : Collection of Vedic hymns.

Śāktism : It conceives *Brahman* or the divine in dynamic terms, and regards energy or power (*śakti*) as intrinsic to the nature of *Brahman* and is the reason for its manifestation in the form of the world.

Sāṁkhya : One of the important schools of Indian philosophy which has influenced all other schools of Indian philosophy.

Smṛti : It refers to the religious literature which is not included in the Śruti tradition.

Spanda : The creative principle intrinsic to the nature of the divine because of which the divine manifests itself in the form of the world.

Upaniṣads : The basic texts of Vedānta, and form part of Śruti.

Upāsanā : Meditation on a deity with a view to achieving something.

Vedānta : The philosophy of the Upaniṣads.

Vimarśa	:	It is that because of which consciousness is self-aware. It is intrinsic to the nature of consciousness
Viṣṇu Purāṇa	:	An important Purāṇic text sacred to Vaiṣṇavism.
Vyāsa	:	The author of *Mahābhārata*, and is known for his attempts to reconcile the traditions of Śruti and Smṛti.

Bibliography

Aitareya-Āraṇyaka, tr. F. Max Müller, The Upaniṣads, Vol. 1, Sacred Books of the East, Delhi: Motilal Banarsidass, 1981.

Bhagavad-Gītā, tr. Franklin Edgerton, Delhi: Motilal Banarsidass, 1996.

Bhāgavata Purāṇa, tr. G.V. Tagare, 5 vols., Ancient Indian Tradition and Mythology Series, Delhi: Motilal Banarsidass, 1987.

Brahma-Sūtras (*Vedānta-Sūtras*) with the commentary of Śaṅkara, tr. by George Thibaut, Sacred Book of the East Series, Delhi: Motilal Banarsidass, in two vols., 1962.

Brahma-Sūtras (*Vedānta-Sūtras*) with the commentary of Rāmānuja known as Śrī Bhāṣya, Sacred Books of the East Series, Delhi: Motilal Banarsidass, 1962.

Bṛhadāraṇyaka Upaniṣad, tr. Swami Madhavananda, Mayavati, Almora: Advaita Ashram, 1950.

Chāndogya Upaniṣad, tr. Swami Gambhirananda, Calcutta: Advaita Ashram, 1983.

Complete Works of Sri Aurobindo, Pondicherry: Sri Aurobindo Ashram, 1972.

Gospel of Sri Ramakrishna, Mylapore, Madras: Ramakrishna Math, 1957.

Life Divine, Pondicherry: Sri Aurobindo Ashram, 1960.

Mahābhārata, tr. Kishori Mohan Ganguli, 12 vols., Delhi: Munshiram Manoharlal, 1976.

Muṇḍaka Upaniṣad, tr. Swami Gambhirananda, Calcutta: Advaita Ashram, 1957.

Ṛgveda Saṁhitā with Sāyaṇa Bhāṣya, 5 vols., Poona: Vaidika Samshodhana Mandala, 1978.

Rumi: Poet and Mystic: Selections from His Writings, tr. Reynold A. Nicholson, London: George Allen and Unwin Ltd., 1956.

Śatapatha Brāhmaṇa, tr. G.J. Eggeling, 5 vols., Sacred Books of the East Series, Delhi: Motilal Banarsidass, 1972.

Śiva-Sūtras, tr. Jaideva Singh, Delhi: Motilal Banarsidass, 2000.

Spanda-Kārikās, tr. Jaideva Singh, Delhi: Motilal Banarsidass, 2000.

Viṣṇu Purāṇa, tr. H.H. Wilson, Calcutta: Punthi Pustak, 1972.

Index